Meandering Mind

Eva Dillner

Books by Eva Dillner
new editions in print, audio and e-book formats

in English
Z 2 A (planned 2010)

Meandering Mind (2010)
1st edition The Pathfinder Process (2005)

3rd edition (planned 2012)
2nd edition Secrets of Transformation (2008)
1st edition The Naked Truth (2003)

Keys to Life Energy (planned 2011)
1st edition God put a Dream in my Heart (2003)

Healing Art Calendar (2010)
Art of Now Calendar (2009)

in Swedish
Våga Leva (2006)
Livs Levande Eva (2006)

Meandering Mind
by Eva Dillner

DIVINE DESIGN
www.divinedesign.nu

Meandering Mind

2nd edition of The Pathfinder Process

originally published by 1st Books/Author House in 2005

Copyright © 2005, 2010 Eva Dillner

Cover painting copyright © 2009 Eva Dillner

ISBN: 978-91-978231-2-8 (6"x9" Softcover)

ISBN: 978-91-977337-9-3 (digital audio)

ISBN: 978-91-978231-1-1 (e-book)

Printed in the UK and USA by Lightning Source

Digital audio available via Audible and Elib

E-book available via Kindle, Elib and Ingram

Published by DIVINE DESIGN

www.divinedesign.nu

Eksjö, Sweden

If you love something

set it free

if it comes back to you

it is yours

if it doesn't

it never was

Table of Contents

One

Rumination pays off

For months I have been chewing on the structure and approach of this book. At first I thought I would write a book with meditations and instructions on how to live life in the flow. But that wasn't it at all, at least not now.

It felt to me as if two books wanted to come through, one on business and one on relationships. Was I meant to write two books side by side? Quite a challenge, one book is quite enough of a project. I pondered the similarities in the books. In both, the premise would be to discover the potential of a group, individual or relationship rather than try to pound people into pre-determined roles and organization charts.

I experienced tremendous resistance to the idea of writing two books simultaneously. Self worth issues surfaced that took me into a very deep and dark place. I questioned once again if writing was really my path. I painted, hoping to unclog the creative flow. How was this to get off the ground?

I puttered with God knows what. I sorted papers, made phone calls, cleaned house, sat and stared into space, put my photo albums in order, played with my computer, daydreamed, had temper tantrums, you name it. I sure wasn't doing any writing. I felt frustrated. I laid on the couch and cried, feeling worthless and unworthy. I just couldn't get going. I could feel the stream of words just waiting to come out my fingertips into the books. But I couldn't find the end of the thread that would start to untangle the whole ball of yarn. I could see the whole ball, lots of threads here and there, all tangled together into a ball. But no start!

Then one day, while I was doing the dishes, the answer fell into place. I had assumed that in being given two subjects I was to make two books. The problem was that I had tried to separate relationships from work, to structure life into some compartmentalized cubes. I didn't live my life that way. My work and relationships intertwine into a whole flow. The two subjects were meant to be in one book. As this thought crystallized in my head, I saw how writing one book could be done as a diary, with one topic following another. I could explore thoughts, experiences and theories without having to have the answers, without having to make a "how to" book. I could be the philosopher that I really am. I could ponder and observe and weave together my blend of life observations into a new whole. I would also have the opportunity to seed new thoughts, to pose new questions as well as share my wisdom. Best of all I wouldn't have to write from an expert point of view, like I knew it all. I could just be myself. What a relief! Yes, that was it!

I want to stimulate you, the reader, into your own exploration and to provide the tools you need, in the book. My goal is to set you free, to help you discover your own inner authority and guidance.

So yes, *rumination* pays off.

What then, do I mean by rumination? I first encountered the term in a book about writing. Unfortunately I don't remember the author or book title, but I do remember the concept. This writer, a woman, had finally created space in her life for writing. Her husband would take the kids on Saturdays so she could write. He would come home and ask, "Honey, what did you write today?" Some days she had not managed to write anything, and she felt tremendous pressure from herself and her husband to produce. He was nice enough to enable her to write, but where was the product?

She finally realized that good writing needs time to come together. That lots of time needs to be spent in what she called rumination. She even got herself a rumination chair. It's where you sit and ponder different approaches and play with thoughts and ideas. You give your mind free reign to explore and wander and wonder.

Once she got her rumination chair, she was at peace when the inevitable question came, "what did you accomplish today?" She could joyfully answer, "I ruminated." And sure enough, the rumination led to writing. Good quality writing.

I suppose that is true with most things - much of the work is done in the preparation. If you are going to paint a house for example, about 80% of the time is preparation work, and only 20% of the time is actually spent on painting.

It's when we let go that the answer comes. I had done all the stewing about how to get the business/relationship books off the ground - then I went to do the dishes and *bingo!* the answer just fell into place. I do believe that the stewing around is just as important to the process as the letting go. So yes, rumination pays off.

How to work with this book

I see my role as a catalyst. I'm an idea generator. I seed new thought. Many of the concepts and ideas I toss out in this book may be new and foreign to you. They may turn your previous beliefs about how things should be upside down. If you find yourself getting upset with some of the ideas, pause, and let your emotions and thoughts percolate for a while. It's ok to stew about it. Notice if you feel resistance or if you find yourself defending your current way of doing things. There are no right or wrong answers.

My hope is to stir your thinking and beliefs, to give you a chance to see things a different way. The solutions to our problems never come from the same level they were created. We have to shift our perspective to see a new solution.

Some ideas are covered more than once. I am aware that there is repetition in this book. It is the way it is supposed to be. If you think about it, when we're exposed to a new idea, we rarely accept it, or even hear it, the first time. New ideas have to be seeded several times before we can take them in. Then we need time to think about them and digest the new material. Only then do we proceed to accept the new thought.

I recommend you read through the book first, then go back through the book a second time and do the exercises. My hope is that you will go back time and time again for many years to come, and that each time you experience a new insight.

Use the exercises that appeal to you. Then, just for kicks, try the ones you really resist. Exploring the very thing you normally wouldn't do, can lead you into some very interesting breakthroughs. You free up a lot of energy by going to that very place you won't allow yourself to go. More on this later.

This book may upset you. You may find yourself questioning your own life. You may vehemently disagree with some of my ideas. You may find some of my views shocking. On the other hand, some of the material may be old hat to you. The ideas in this book are my own. I have no wish to force them on you. I offer my ideas as seeds for pondering. Take what works and leave the rest.

May I teach the exercises in this book?

Not long ago, one of my colleagues asked for permission to teach an exercise from my first book. I was elated she liked the exercises. *Of course you may teach anything that is written about in my books!* I want you to. I encourage you to incorporate ideas and exercises into your own practice, for whatever reason. Just be sure to mention where you found the exercises. Whether you are a consultant, teacher, therapist or manager, please feel free to adapt the material as you see fit. Refer your students to my books. Knowledge is not static. It grows and develops when we use it. As we use it the understanding changes. This is the natural flow of life.

Two

A woman on a mission

My spiritual name is *Pathfinder*. My mission in life is to find new paths, to discover new ways to do things, to seek new solutions, to meander down a different path than the traditional one. I was a groundbreaker in business as one of the first women engineers in the paper industry so it should not be so surprising that I have a different approach to relationships and organizations. If you're looking for traditional ideas and models for organizations and relationships, then this book is not for you.

I don't believe in cookie cutter formulas or rigid step-by-step proce-dures. I do believe in living, breathing, changeable processes. I want to give you the tools to do your own thinking, feeling and analysis. Each case is unique and has it's own unique solution. So this book is about discovering new paths, new ways to look at relationships and organi-zations with much help along the way to stimulate and expand your thinking.

Organizations are relationships

This may be a new concept for you, that *organizations are relation-ships*. We traditionally think of relationships as love relationships, such as in marriage or relationships with children, siblings or parents. Truth is we have many different kinds of relationships, which form our experience of life. We have relationships with friends, with neighbors, with colleagues, with clients, with suppliers as well as with clerks at stores. Some relationships may be at the level of exchanging a few nice-ties across the counter, others plunge much deeper depths and last for lifetimes.

Perhaps you are used to thinking in terms of organization charts, where there are boxes with people's names and titles in them. These organization charts are often hierarchical in nature and problems arise when the natural energy flow between people is inhibited.

"Natural energy flow,?" you ask. Well, I see organizations as living organisms with a natural energy flow. If you organize the work in a natural way, the organization functions at its optimal level. I will give plenty of examples of this as we go along.

For an organization to perform well, the relationships within it have to be functional. Unfortunately, we bring all our baggage and dysfunctions to work and many organizations are hell to work for these days. I call it *managing to mediocrity*. It is this way only because there is a limited understanding of how it all works.

Relationships are organizations. You can't have one without the other. Whenever two or more people get together it's an organization, even if it's only two friends getting together for dinner or a movie. Families are organizations. Social events are organizations. Our relationships form our work organizations.

Stunned into silence

I would have written this book a long time ago, but there have been obstacles in the way. There has been a lot to work through therapeutically. I have published two books on therapy and personal growth. But the book you are holding in your hands is the one I wanted to write first.

I had completed a fifteen-year corporate career with an assignment in France. We spent two years building a new factory. It was an intense and difficult project in any language and culture. We pulled it off on schedule and under budget and had really done a terrific job. My boss wrote a promotion recommendation for me, got it signed off by the entire European management team and sent it off to my boss-to-be at headquarters, who put it in his desk drawer.

My new boss made it crystal clear he could care less what I had been up to in France. He refused to even look at the promotion recommendation. He just put it aside, with no interest whatsoever. I was stunned. I was speechless. At the time there were so many things to deal with that I glossed over it emotionally. That's what happens when you get a shock. Your system shuts down and with it the emotions get buried. Complicating the problem was my wish to continue with international work and our company was closing the international division. I was also getting strong signals from my body that I needed to take a break.

I had been going non-stop at a fairly intense pace since I started university, where I carried a heavy course load. I went straight to work when I finished my Master's degree. I had wanted to take time out during my studies, but my practical parents convinced me to wait until I graduated. Turned out it was practically impossible then, you might as well throw your degree away if you took a time out.

So there I was twenty years later, feeling like I needed a break, my new boss didn't want me and there were no exciting projects on the horizon.

I had been toying with the idea of writing. In my mind I saw myself writing books. I was terrified to just quit outright. I asked for a leave of absence for three months. At the end of those three months, my boss, the one who didn't want me in the first place, called to tell me I had been laid off.

But back to the stunned into silence. It's now fifteen years later and I have finally uncorked the emotional trauma at not being seen or acknowledged by my new boss. I know I'm not alone. The damage done to people in organizations that downsize, restructure and reshuffle is enormous. There is a whole army of emotionally crippled people out there trying to hold their lives together. Can you imagine what a different world it would be if we could take our issues into therapy and resolve them as we go?

Had I been emotionally whole at the time, I could have stood up for myself, said how I felt and dealt with the emotional pain of being ignored. My accomplishments are very important to me. Obviously, the whole European management team thought I had done a very good job. It was beyond my comprehension that you could just ignore such a glowing recommendation. Perhaps he was jealous or it reminded him of a sister who got all the attention, who knows? Point is, it hurt me tremendously. I experienced excruciating low back pain, my root chakra locked up and I developed uterine fibroids. My whole sense of self had been invalidated. This end-of-career incident wasn't the only one that contributed to my difficulties, but it was a major one.

Unfortunately there are few therapists who understand how to work with work and organizational trauma. Their training and experience tends to focus on traditional relationship issues and physical traumas. For more information on how to work therapeutically with life's difficulties, see my other books. In these books you will also find many useful exercises for personal and spiritual growth.

I took a long rest after being let go from my corporate job. Then I started writing. I titled my book *Managing to Mediocrity*. After all, that was my experience. So much garbage went on that had nothing to do with doing a good job or making profits for the company. With all the reorganizations it was every man (or woman) for himself with lots of petty politics and behind the scenes manipulations. However, I didn't get very far with my writing, at that time...

Managing to mediocrity

In many countries there's been a reality show on TV called *Survivor*. The competitors go to an island and are pitted against each other individually and in teams, in survival and other games. Each week a loser has to leave the island until there is only the winner left. You would think that the strongest or most capable would win. Not so. In the early stages, the competition is between teams. The focus is on cooperation and support, so that the team can win. At this stage it's the weaker participants who end up leaving. Then the competition turns individual. Each to his or her own. Now the game is to get rid of the strong ones, so there is less competition at the end. As one astute winner said, "the trick is to hang in there while not looking like a threat to anyone." Quite the opposite of being capable or strong.

So the fittest don't win. Much like it has become in the corporate world. It's not about being capable. It's about blending in and making it to the top. To make it easier to advance, you work to get rid of anyone who looks better than you do in the accomplishment arena. In other words the system produces *managing to mediocrity*.

It makes me very sad to think of all the talent that is sidelined, not because they are not capable, but because they are perceived to be a threat to those who want to climb the ladder. It's a very sick system. My goal is not to belabor what is wrong in the world, but rather to show ways we can make organizations and relationships right again. I'm sure it was the Divine plan that I not write this book when all I could see was managing to mediocrity. I needed to grow and develop first. The book I'm writing now is about *transformation*, how to release what doesn't work and introduce new ways of being and doing at home and at work.

Three

Imposing beliefs

To make matters worse, during my first go at making a career out of writing, a friend of mine called one night. She had been thinking, she said, and had reached the conclusion that I wasn't meant to be a writer. Her belief was that writers are obsessed with writing, they carry pen and paper wherever they go, they are fired up about their subject matter and they write easily, the words just come pouring out. I didn't fit that mold. She spent two hours on the telephone *imposing her belief* on me that I shouldn't write. I didn't have enough sense to tell her to go pound sand. I had enough doubts of my own - all writers do and sometimes the internal critic gets very loud. After that two hour pounding I put away my writing and started a long search for what I was meant to do. Little did I understand how lost I was.

My friend imposed her beliefs on me. One of the things I would like to change in the world is a) that we stop taking on other people's garbage and b) that we stop imposing our beliefs on others.

Recently I have been working through the exercises from Carmen Harra's book *Everyday Karma*. In reviewing all the love relationships I had had, whether brief or extended, it became plain that I had cleared the emotional pain from my encounters. What remained were judgments I had about myself based on beliefs imposed by others.

Projections

In therapy speak, when we impose our beliefs on others, it is called *projection*. In other words, my friend who didn't think I should be a writer projected her beliefs on me based on what it meant to be a writer for her. What she was really saying was that if she were to be a writer she would need to be obsessed with writing. Perhaps this was true for her, but it sure wasn't for me. If she had said, "this is what I believe it means to be a writer," then we could have had a dialogue about it. It would have been nice if she could have been supportive of me trying out a new career. Chances are she had been squashed in what she really wanted to do and was just passing on the favor, so to speak. We tend to unconsciously repeat what has been done to us, until we clear it up therapeutically. Then we heal not only ourselves, we help move the entire planet along. That's how important each and every one of our actions is.

In looking back at my relationships, I carried a lot of projections and imposed beliefs from others about what was ok and not ok. It was their beliefs and their projections, but I had taken them on as my own. Let me give you a few examples, and there are lots as my relationship history includes some fifty men. Yikes you say! Fifty, did she really say fifty! Yep, that's right. And one woman. You probably wonder why I would include such embarrassing statistics about myself. Me too. But I have discovered that it's only embarrassing as long as you keep it a secret, something to not be talked about, something to keep hushed up. Letting it out into the open frees up my energy and what was a big issue becomes a non-issue. I mean, how much fun is it to berate someone who just stands there and says, yeah, you got it right. I said fifty men and one woman.

Furthermore, I have discovered that many other women have had similar experiences, and have been made to feel less acceptable for it. So partly it's to help free them up as well, to make it ok. If I was a man and made the same statement, you'd slap me on the back and wink at me, "way to go!" like I had achieved something to be proud of. Well who do you think all the Casanovas are getting it on with? Not themselves, that's for sure.

Now you probably wonder how many one-night stands I've had? Only three, actually, the rest showed up for more. Included in the three was the one woman. We'd had a bit to drink, we were young and she said, "I've always been curious what it would be like to make love to a woman. Logically we should know how to please each other." I agreed. It was a small risk to take and I felt ok about it, as I knew she was as crazy about men as I was. It was an ok experience. We both agreed it had been an interesting exercise and that we needn't do it again.

I have taken a lot of heat from well meaning friends about my sexual appetite. They have thought it wrong to just enjoy the physical, that for a relationship to have meaning it must last and lead somewhere and one shouldn't jump into bed until one has a commitment. I agree relationships are nice if they have depth, where you can talk to each other, you can emote and support each other, you have common interests and so on.

But each relationship has a different purpose. Just look at your circle of friends. With some friends you share one interest, with others it's something else. Some friendships last a lifetime, others just a short while. They are what they are.

A friend of mine went to a psychic a few years ago. She was at the time in a relationship that was very physical, but she wanted more. The psychic told her, "no, this one is for your body. He is very good for your body. You think you want more, but that is not what he is for in your life." Hearing this helped my friend let go of what her mind was trying to impose as the way it should be. She relaxed and let herself enjoy the love affair of her life. It was true, this man was very good for her body.

Four

Bambi on ice

How many times have we not allowed ourselves to do, or feel, or be, what we really wanted? We have so many taboos and so many "not alloweds." But if you think about it, our rules are made up by our minds. Customs vary from culture to culture. What is considered normal or acceptable deviates a lot by culture. So to my way of thinking, it's our heads that try to make up the rules. But that may go against what our bodies tell us or our Spiritual self guides us to do.

A woman friend had the dilemma of what to do with the infatuation of a male acquaintance. She was living with her boyfriend and enjoyed this other male as a friend. As their friendship deepened, he fell in love with her. At first she felt panicked, "how do I deal with this? I am not in love with him, I have my live-in boyfriend, help, what do I do?" My viewpoint was to not do anything, to simply allow the friend to express and experience his attraction to her. She need not respond or return the feelings. She could simply be clear in her response that she cared about him as a friend. By letting the feelings come to the surface, by acknowledging them and letting them blossom, his infatuation can bloom out and clear the path for them to have a close friendship. There was nothing secret or hidden about it. I believe we create more problems when we don't allow ourselves to feel what we really feel. When we shut off what we really feel we create tension.

Love isn't some limited quantity. It's unlimited. I love all my friends in a different way. The more we can love ourselves, the more we are free to love one another. A parent's love for a child is different than brother-sister love or romantic love. The love in marriage may be quite different than a brief love affair, but it's all about love.

Take a look at your rulebook. What is allowed? What is crazy? What is not allowed? What is not permitted? Who decides? Why do you have these rules? What is the purpose of your rules? What would happen if you broke your rules, or changed them?

One of the concepts I am exploring in this book is that we cause a lot of problems in relationships and business by trying to pound each other into predetermined roles, instead of exploring who we really are. If we could focus on discovering our respective potentials, then look at where we can intersect we would be miles ahead. The trick then is letting go of the rest. Square pegs and round holes are only imaginary boundaries, mere constructs of our mental prisons.

But how do you go about getting to know each other and discovering how and where you are meant to intersect? Well, I had the opportunity to test part of my theory on a man I met. Here is an email I sent him on this very subject:

Hello,

Yesterday I took quite a tumble, didn't realize there was black ice under the snow I was walking on - and landed flat on my back. Like "Bambi on ice," if you've seen the Disney movie. Needless to say it shook me up, amazingly enough I didn't break anything and walked away without a bruise. I have a friend who does this on a regular basis, her helpers make her tumble or fall but in the process they open her up to another way to see the world. I feel like I had a chiropractic adjustment courtesy of my helpers, angels or guides, or whatever you want to call them.

Last night I dreamt a lot and went off to tropical paradises and islands and God knows what. I woke up with the certainty it's time to revisit Tenerife. When I was there a few years ago I fell in love with it and was all ready to move there to the north side, Puerto de la Cruz - but all of a sudden the universe put a stop to that. At the time I was training to become an instructor in Shen therapy, that organization fell apart, my heart wasn't in teaching therapy and then I started writing books...

I suppose this is where you come in ... you may wonder where you fit in ... so do I.

Ever since I met you, I've wondered why you are in my life. At first I wanted to slot you in, define it, my mind wanted to know. I could see you as a friend, a lover, a relationship, a colleague, someone to do therapy with etc. You could potentially fill a lot of roles, none or some or a combination?????

My Higher Self simply said - be present - and see what happens. Instead of trying to define life, just let it happen, you don't need to analyze or understand or define. Just explore the present. Be true to yourself and communicate from that place.

I still don't know why you are in my life. All I can say is I am curious, I like talking to you and sure there is a physical attraction but maybe that isn't what this is about. From our chats I know you too have had lots of experience being the "pleasure source." Of the many men I've been with there haven't been many that have been interested in knowing who I really was, and truthfully I may not have let them past my defenses. I don't know if I'm making much sense here. I've been thinking a lot about how difficult it can be to get beyond what we imagine the other person really is about. My friend and I have had lots of dialogue on this - men fall in love with her and want to take care of her, but they don't really see her. At least when I was younger, men would want to have sex with me, but didn't really see me. I don't know if this is true for you, but I can imagine that women would want you, but have not a clue who you really are.

Anyhow, I decided I need to take a trip to Tenerife. And I know you like sea and sun. Here is a window of opportunity - do you want to come along? If you do, I would like this to be without expectations, I honestly don't know what I want other than to get to know you better. We may spend the entire time talking, what I'm trying to say is I don't know if my body is going to want sex or not - I can't believe I'm saying this. I'd like us to meet without scripts and expectations and preconceived ideas of what this is about. And this way there is no pressure on either one of us, we are free to be ourselves and not live up to some role. You may have some ground rules that are important to you.

Ah yes, nothing ventured, nothing gained...

Better send this before I lose my nerve

Eva

A new sense of freedom invaded my space. Only a few days earlier, I had purchased a new charm for my bracelet - the Statue of Liberty - or as she is called in Swedish *the Goddess of Freedom*. I felt free. I was exploring new territory. I allowed myself to think about my rule "one man at a time." Was I really serially monogamous, could I be interested in more than one man at a time? Was my rule the real me, or just some imposed thought that I had swallowed hook line and sinker.

A letter arrived from a friend of a friend - a man seeking contact, an artist, who maybe could be of interest? As a friend or whatever? I pondered how we assume that one precludes the other. That life is an *either/or* instead of this *and* that. Like the subjects of this book, the assumption is that business and relationships are two topics and need to be separated, that somehow one precludes the other. I can do corporate career work, that doesn't preclude me from being a writer or an artist. If I love one person it doesn't mean I can't love someone else. Love is not a finite quantity that will run out.

In Shirley MacLaine's movie *Out on a Limb*, her lover admits the problem is he does not love himself enough. And Shirley offers the insight that if he loved himself more, he would be free to love his wife, he would be free to love her, and he would be free to love his work and his children. So why do we assume that love is a finite quantity that has to be hoarded and doled out like rations?

With this newfound sense of freedom, I kept sorting material for this book. I was going through some of my career stuff and ran across a name of someone I had worked with in the past. Believing in taking action when inspired I surfed Google and sure enough, I found his email address. Isn't the internet great? Off went an email with "Hi how are you?"

I went to a painting weekend. There is something deeper that happens with your process when you paint in a group. This weekend was special too as the founder of Vedic Art, Curt Källman, was introducing expanded aspects of the basic principles. The first day I piddled with details and was just there, hanging out. Day two I brought my acrylic paints and as so often happens, when you let go, magic happens. I came home with a painting ready to frame. I felt really pleased. It's when you aren't focused on accomplishing that the magic happens, when you let your feelings and consciousness take over and become the painting. It's true of any process. I'm being danced or written or painted. I've sent my critic brain on vacation. I think magic happens when we are whole brained, the two halves are connected and working in sync.

It's that space in between, some artists call it negative space. I think it's the same with all creativity. It happens between the left and the right brain.

Talking dog exercise

I wanted to introduce this exercise early on as it is key in creating dialogue. It's actually an adaptation of the American Indian way of communicating called *talking stick*. Whoever holds the stick has the word and everyone else listens. To lighten up the exercise I've used a stuffed animal such as a Dalmatian puppy, thereof the name *talking dog*. You can use anything, a paperweight, a teddy bear, a crystal, whatever strikes your fancy.

Many of us use this method while on courses. But how many practice it in their everyday lives? Not many, and that holds true for me too. Perhaps it is time to take all the wonderful tools we have learned at all the wonderful workshops we have attended into our everyday not so wonderful lives? To take the learning one step further, into our lives. Let's start practicing the methods at home and at work.

For the *talking dog exercise* you first need to agree on the object to use as a talking dog. Then sit in a circle or around a table. Put the talking dog in the center between you. Take a few moments to quiet yourself, take a few deep breaths and center yourself here and now. Let the days interferences go and focus on being true to yourself in the moment. Each one sits quietly until stirred to speak. When you feel stirred to speak, you pick up the talking dog. Sit with the dog and let yourself be guided to speak, from your heart and your deepest self. Communicate honestly and as free as you can. It's ok to be silent, to take all the time you need. Sometimes you pick up the talking dog and just sit there in silence. When you feel there is no more to be said, put the puppy back in the center.

As one speaks, the others listen. No interruptions are allowed. Focus on listening, hearing and understanding what is being said. Be here now. Don't worry about what you are going to say. Listen to the person speaking. Be here now. Really take in what is being said. If you want the speaker to clarify something, you have to wait your turn as the speaker.

Each time the puppy goes back in the center, wait and see if someone else picks it up. Keep going until the talking stops. There will be a natural ending when all that needed to be said at this time has been said and it's time to close the circle.

Keep this exercise in mind where I suggest you dialogue about your discoveries. For many of the exercises in this book there is an individual part to be done first, followed by a couple or group exercise with dialogue and sharing. Using the talking dog principles will help you get much more out of the dialogue as it makes sure each person gets their input heard and seen.

Five

Puzzle pieces

Have you ever tried to put together a puzzle without knowing what the picture is supposed to look like when it's finished? Of course not, that's not how we do it.

There is an experiment described in Jane Hundley's book *The Power of Personal Presence* that illustrates the importance of having a clear picture of what the puzzle is supposed to look like. It doesn't matter if you are talking about a regular puzzle or an organization's strategic vision or something in between, the principle is the same. You have to have an idea of what the end product is supposed to look like, to agree on where you are headed or you will be pulling in different directions and not understand why. This applies to relationships where the partners may have totally different values and end goals, or organizations where each participant has their own idea of what it's supposed to look like when they are done.

First, let me describe the puzzle experiment. Then, we'll get back to looking at the implications and applications of the puzzle principle. Jane calls this process *Mental Rehearsal*:

"The power of mental rehearsal in organizing group thought is profound. An executive tested the idea about group vision. To a group of employees, he gave a puzzle to put together. He told no one what the final picture was supposed to look like. They could not solve the puzzle or put pieces in their place. Then he took one employee at a time into his office, and showed each one a different picture of the completed picture. This produced group confusion, tension and frustration. Then he showed them all at once what the final picture would look like. He gave them the same vision. They put the puzzle pieces together in no time at all."

from *The Power of Personal Presence* by Jane Hundley

This concept was forcefully brought home to me when I got involved with the Swedish Cultural Center in Seattle. In it's heyday they had 10,000 members, which by now had dwindled to a few thousand. The Club owned a three-story building complete with restaurant, bar, banquet facilities, meeting rooms and parking lots in a great location with beautiful views of Lake Union and the Seattle skyline. What they lacked was a new purpose, the country club days were over.

As this was a volunteer organization, it was important to tap the enthusiasm of the members. In a corporation you can to a certain extent impose your will on the drones, but it's simply not possible when you are dealing with volunteers.

There were a number of willing contributors, with lots of ideas on how to revive the Club. It was obvious to me that the end vision varied immensely between the participants. One person would describe images of a very upscale club attracting the well to do. Another talked in terms of IKEA furnishings. A third would talk about family activities. A fourth would push large scale fund raising as the road to salvation. Yet another would have ideas for low cost activities to bring people into the club. No wonder they seemed to be pulling in different directions - they were.

Be true to yourself

In a moment we'll explore how a group can create a common vision that includes the potential and passion of the individuals. But first I want to share a few more examples of uncommon end goals and the problems they create.

I need go no further than my crashed marriage. Sure we had a lot of other problems, but the underlying source of tension was that we wanted different things out of life.

When I met my ex, I was in graduate school heading for a Master's Degree in Mechanical Engineering. I wanted to travel, see the world and make good money. He was six years older than I, smart, very intelligent, he loved the outdoors and he'd chosen to work in the woods. His ambition in life? Hard to say, he kept talking about moving out into a cabin in the woods. He wanted to write and kept prodding me to quit my job. I think he would have been happy with a hippie lifestyle. We made the mistake so many people do, we fell into the trap of what it's supposed to look like when you are in love. We got married, bought a house and life went from bad to worse. Neither one of us was true to ourselves.

Had I been true to myself, I would have taken the best job, not the one that kept me in Seattle. See, he didn't want to move. I was in love and didn't want to leave him. Same old story, give up your true desires and you lose yourself. He didn't want to settle down and make money and be responsible. He wanted to play and drink and get by. He had no desire to travel. Had we been able to talk about values and expectations and had the inner freedom to be true to ourselves, we could have had a totally different outcome. There is no guarantee the relationship would have been any better, but we wouldn't have sacrificed ourselves, and for what? The financial responsibilities drove him nuts, he didn't want to be responsible. I was frustrated because I wasn't living the independent life I wanted. Truth is I was scared to be alone. Not a good basis for getting married.

In hindsight - it's always 20/20 isn't it? - I should have taken my fearful self off into the world, and let go of him. Who knows, we may have continued a long distance romance that may have been something really special. We'll never know.

We both bought into the idea of owning property but neither one of us was interested in all that goes with it. You know, maintaining a yard, fixing leaky faucets or spending your weekends doing home improvement projects. We would have been much better off as renters, free to pursue other interests. He was an excellent cook. We shared a love of music and reading. He could have lived in the woods and I could have taken off on my international jaunts. Point is, we didn't try to find the intersection of our lives, and neither one of us was true to our real desires. We didn't have the same values and goals for our lives.

The Headline Game

So how do you discover if you have a future in common? There is an exercise called the *headline game* that I learned at an EU Network seminar. It was presented as an organization tool, but it could be used for relationships as well. Because it highlights your inner wishes it provides a focus for dialogue.

While ruminating on this book, I was asked to help a therapy organization with their strategy and vision. I began an email interactive, iterative correspondence with the instructors and business minds of the organization. To summarize the work and to engage the entire membership in the process I wrote an article for their newsletter. I have included some of it here as it so well illustrates the headline game process. To make the exercise more universal I used ABC instead of the therapy name. As you read through, just insert your own life issue into the exercise.

Vision and Strategy

Your President asked me to help out on the strategic thinking for ABC. In the first go around we involved a smaller group consisting mainly of instructors. This has helped start the process and dialogue. I see this as an iterative process and would like to involve the entire membership. In this way we can really tap the potential of the whole group and I believe it will stimulate dialogue and get the creative juices flowing to really get ABC out there in the world in a way that is synergistic with the people actually doing it.

Typically we think of strategy and vision statements as a top down thing - something that is the territory of an elite few. But I believe that a vision that is formed by tapping the passion of the entire organization is a much more powerful force. Because everyone is part of the plan, and is involved in creating it. When we get to work for ideas and ideals that are close to our hearts, we are truly motivated.

For a start, I reviewed the documents - Business Plan, First Thoughts on a Strategy and Articles of Association. The amount of work put in over the years to move ABC forward is considerable and in the process much wisdom has been gathered. Putting my thinking cap on and letting inspiration work it's magic I sent out my first request:

My hope is to harvest your collective wisdom into a clear strategy and vision for ABC. Once the goal is clear, the detail business planning at the local level can fall into place easily. I look at it a bit like laying a puzzle, you need to have an idea what it's supposed to look like before you can put it together.

Let's start with the assumption that anything is possible. What is your deepest wish for ABC? What, in your wildest fantasy could happen? What legacy would you like to leave with ABC at the center?

A fun exercise to get in touch with possible visions, is what I call the headline game. Imagine it's five, ten or twenty years into the future. What headline do you see in the news about ABC? If you like to draw or meditate, utilize those tools to help you get in touch with your imagination mind. Ask yourself, from the deepest part of your soul, what am I to be a part of? What wants to happen with ABC? Then jot down the headlines that pop into your mind. As with any brainstorming, ask your censoring mind to go on vacation. Our analytical minds will have plenty to do later when we get into the detail planning. Now the focus is on vision, strategy, dreaming and ideas. So let your creative self dream and send me back one or more headlines, as many as you wish. Then we'll have an iterative discussion to hone those imaginations into a cohesive whole. An ABC Vision!

Never mind what you think it should be - what is in your heart? Where is your passion with ABC? What excites you? Where is your growth with ABC? Look ahead, if you could choose any role to play in ABC, what would you focus on and what headline would describe that?

Here are the headlines that came back in the first go-around:

- "ABC changed my life," say 50 of the world's most influential leaders
- ABC wins award for most innovative and inspiring training
- Demand for ABC therapy at all time high, as people delve deeper into their emotional lives
- ABC opens 30th worldwide centre, where anyone can drop in for information or training services
- "I can't believe there are still people out there who haven't heard of ABC," says Dalai Lama
- "ABC has influenced reduction in worldwide conflict," say top researchers
- ABC courses offered at local school for single parents
- ABC is offered to all crime, abuse and accident victims as a matter of course
- ABC will be paid for on the National Health
- New therapy to take the world by storm
- ABC Therapy: Discover how people are being empowered
- Wonderful therapy that allows people to take control of their lives
- Are you brave enough to face your demons? Find out with ABC!!
- What next after Reiki? Take a look at ABC, the stars' favourite therapy
- "ABC Therapy really changes peoples lives for the better," says Top Psychiatrist
- ABC can pave the way towards greater spiritual development
- ABC is the treatment of choice for patients with Post Traumatic Stress Disorder
- Research demonstrates Effectiveness of ABC

- ABC is becoming one of the most sought after therapies

WOW - now there is a lot of excitement! To me, this is the fun part of business planning. My follow-up to the initial group:

Now, as we look at these, what emerges? What more would you like to add? Certainly there is a quest to get ABC recognized, documented and into the system. And to help people grow and heal.

I would like you all to ponder, where is my energy in all this? Do I want to focus on doing the work? Helping as many people as I can? Help a few people go really far? Teaching? Do I want to train therapists or teach people to work on each other? Do research? Focus on making ABC a licensable profession? Create dynamite training materials and processes? These are just some ideas to get you started. If you, personally, could do one thing with ABC, what would it be? Where would you focus your energy? I want to hear where your individual passions lie.

The passion responses that came back really illustrate the diverse values that are contained in the whole of ABC:

- I see us writing books about our work and going on talk shows like Oprah's. I see this work be used in prisons and hospitals. And I see it especially be used to support all humankind to become totally peaceful, internally.

- My passion is to get ABC to be increasingly effective with clients.

- Here's my vision: to have ABC Therapy be a household word, to have ABC be as commonly used in every household as a broom or vacuum. That is, I want to develop curricula of introductory ABC techniques, which we can teach everyone, starting with 6-year-old kids. Every household would think in terms of energy healing FIRST, not last, eventually the pharmaceutical companies would go out of business, as people would see the effectiveness and Cost-Effectiveness of the Maintenance-of-Health model, as opposed to the Suppression-of-Symptoms model.

- The deep emotional work would be done by certified people, of course, but, with enough of the lower level work out there, the "net contraction quotient" in the population would be on the decline. In two generations, the shift from competition to cooperation would be accomplished, nation states will become an anachronism, as the need for global community is met with receptivity rather than fear.

- Correlatively, I want to continue to develop the model we have, to do structured research on a number of relevant health issues, train as many practitioners as is possible, and develop ways of training more practitioners at a time. Phew!

YES and YIPPEE!!!

In reading your feedback I feel truly blessed to be working with such powerful ideas and ideals. You're wonderful!

I would like to see this article published with a call for feedback and dialogue from the members. From there we can start to form networks sorted by passions, as it were. My experience, especially with volunteer organizations, is to focus on where the enthusiasm takes root and drop the rest. We may have 100 ideas but only 5 ignite enthusiasm where someone says, "I really want to work on that." Those are the 5 ideas we focus on now. Later on, we can revisit the other 95 ideas and see if it's time to move forward on them.

Now take your own organization or situation and apply the headline game. What crazy or sane ideas pop into your head? Let your imagination soar, like the therapists did in the above example, and see what you come up with. You may be surprised. Even if only one idea comes to fruition out of it you will have profited from the exercise.

Six

What do you do?

In digging out material for this book, I've revisited resumes, recommendation letters and write-ups I've done during my job searches. A resume shows what you've done, where you've already been. What it doesn't show is how you go about doing what you do, what your MO, or *modus operandi* is, to achieve results. It felt a natural part of my writing process to redo my resume, just one more time, to help pull together where I had been. I won't bore you with the details here, but it was an interesting exercise that helped move the writing of this book forward.

Putting together your CV or presentation is a way to connect with where you've been and helps to highlight your skills and accomplishments.

When people have looked at my resume and my diverse experience, there is one question I get more than any other "what is your area?" followed by "is it engineering or purchasing or budgeting or...?" We are taught to think in terms of professional areas, which are useful at the level where you need to be a specialist, such as in accounting, or in engineering design. But when you deal with project management and broader logistics issues, there are qualities that reach across the boundaries of traditional departments.

Looking at what you do in a different perspective can help you see where your special talent lies. When I was an engineering supervisor, I had six project engineers working for me. If you looked at their resumes you would see that they were all accomplished at doing project management in a tissue mill. But their particular talents varied. One would be very good at keeping track of the cost management, another was creative in finding technical solutions, another really excelled when there was a crisis, yet another possessed the steadfastness to hang in there year after year with all the ups and downs of the business.

So each one of us brings our special gift to whatever we do. I seem to have a knack for change, for seeing new ways to do things organization-ally, to tap the energy of whatever I'm involved with. I see organizations as energy, life energy, and it's just a matter of organizing the work to align with where the energy is and the results take care of themselves. Well, almost, it isn't quite as flippantly simple as that. Usually there is a lot of stewing around before I get there, lest you think I just wave a magic wand and *presto!* life is wonderful.

Seven

Getting to the heart of the matter

Back when I was actively job hunting, I was asked the "what do you do?" question so often I finally got tired of it. I sat down to analyze my work. Was there a common thread? Well, yes, of course there was. It didn't reveal itself immediately. It took a fair amount of digging and sorting and analyzing. I will get back to the process I used to arrive at my common thread in a bit.

But first. I was so excited when I discovered there were certain elements that I used, over and over again. I called the process re-engineering, a newly coined term in 1994, as it most closely matched what I naturally did. I had been doing it for a long time, only the term re-engineering was new. A former colleague once exclaimed, "Eva, your middle name is change!"

Here is the pamphlet I put together with my newly discovered wisdom:

Fundamentals of Re-Engineering

What does a re-engineering manager do?
Organizes work around individual strengths so that minimum effort yields maximum results for the team. Pares down work to essentials, then adds enough of a human touch to make the work fun. Connects the "dots" in new ways by networking people and information in the most direct and efficient manner. Dives into uncharted waters exploring visions of a new matrix.

What makes an ideal climate for re-engineering?
Top management has set a strategic direction that rewards re-engineering efforts. There is responsibility, autonomy and authority to implement changes in organization, processes and procedures. The company has a

long term focus, invests for the future by treating employees, suppliers and customers fairly, maintains and improves physical assets, conducts their business with honesty, ethics and integrity, encourages employees to be innovative and creative and rewards them for doing the right things.

Why re-engineer?
In today's global business climate, you can't afford not to. Re-engineering is the art and the science of transforming an organization at the core so that a shift to the next level of excellence can be achieved. It is about making the company more profitable and ensuring its continuation well into the next millennium.

Ground rules
No idea is too crazy to be considered. Everyone affected is asked for input. Show respect for each individual - you can learn more by listening than by talking. Try not to judge ideas as good or bad, but allow the ideas to evolve. Inherent in the creative process is the dissolution or falling apart of the old form. Be willing and open to let go of old belief systems and behavior patterns that no longer serve you. From physics, we know that order is preceded by chaos. Nature teaches us that to become a butterfly the caterpillar must pass through a chrysalis state.

Step 1 - Learn
Like any problem, you need to define it before you can solve it. How is the work accomplished now and why? What is the actual process? How does this compare to the written down process? Why is this work being done? How does this work support the strategic, long-term vision of the company as well as what is it contributing today? What are the soft benefits, e.g. customer satisfaction, building and maintaining relationships, goodwill in the community? What are the hard benefits in dollar terms? What are the key skills of the people doing the work - are they using their best skills and doing what they do best? It is important to get an overview, to see the forest before analyzing the trees.

Step 2 - Build relationships
While researching in step one, a parallel process is the building of relationships. To make fundamental shifts that last, individual people need to participate in the process. If you are going to change someone's job, they need to feel a part of the solution and you need them on your team to be a successful implementer. What you are aiming for is that all affected have ownership of the process, understand the potentials, and feel that they have been listened to, that their ideas are taken seriously. Don't forget to connect with the quiet ones, they frequently have the best ideas.

Step 3 - Brainstorm

List all possible improvements. At this point, make no judgments about feasibility or effectiveness. Be playful, be creative. Try to expand your thinking. Listen to your intuition. Be audacious. If you were starting from scratch, how would you design and organize the work? How can work be streamlined or rebundled, who really needs to be involved? Who is the most appropriate person to make what decisions? Who should best handle what work? What can be eliminated? Where is the garden in need of weeding and pruning? How can "dots" be connected in new ways? How can work be organized to draw on key skills of employees? Is there new technology or new tools available that could be implemented for efficiency gains? How could cross pollenization between departments help? Bring fresh viewpoints, new thinking, change in attitude. Brainstorm with the awareness that nobody knows it all.

Step 4 - Prioritize

Which ideas have the biggest payoff? What is the relative difficulty and cost of implementing changes? Will the effect be seen only this quarter or is the change enduring? For example, cutting R&D spending today improves quarterly results but makes no sense for a company that wants to be in business long term. Is there one idea that has popular support that would be easy to implement which could start the process and build goodwill? Use discernment.

Step 5 - Analyze

This is the trees part. Document where you are now. Analyze potential benefits, soft and hard. What alternatives are there? What is the bottom line impact of keeping inefficient systems?

Step 6 - Plan & Organize

Put together the plan for projects, key decision points, target dates, key resources needed etc. Obtain approval for issues beyond function jurisdiction. Ideally, the Re-Engineering Manager is put in charge of the function to be re-engineered. This ensures that he or she has the authority to implement changes.

Step 7 - Implement

Depending on alternatives pursued, this phase may be long or short. What you learn from the implementation phase forms the basis for the next level of improvements. Learn to see both the forest and the trees. The learning is on-going. Return to step one and remember - the joy is in the journey!

Examples of re-engineering

- Eliminated 75% of reports previously generated that were found to be non-essential.

- Increased quality levels and streamlined communications by connecting users directly with producers at shop floor level.

- Reduced development cycle time 60% from concept to finished product by discovering real instead of written processes and procedures, by streamlining communication flows, by upgrading capability of people involved in the material flow chain, by learning the supplier manufacturing processes to understand what information they needed at what time and in what form. Sales volume went from zero to one million cases per year.

- Increased engineering staff productivity 10% by developing new planning model for prioritizing and assigning projects.

About the Author

Ms. Dillner graduated with honors from the University of Washington with BS and MS degrees in mechanical engineering and readily passed the professional engineering license exam. True to her INTJ type, she has always sought to find more effective ways to accomplish work. She has a fifteen-year track record of achievement in management roles reaching across packaging, purchasing, engineering and international construction for a Fortune 500 manufacturing company. Her studies of creativity, intuition and the theories of individual working and learning styles add another dimension to her competence.

What others say

"...thanks for your professionalism, dedication and determination to bring the value of our department to the high level it now enjoys..."

"...a self starter developing systems and methods to increase efficiency and organization..."

"...excellent delegator with a strong emphasis on personal growth..."

"...extremely well organized and very efficient at prioritizing..."

"...has the ability to get to the heart of a problem..."

Squashed by projections

Sound pretty good, doesn't it? One of my "life energy" friends liked it a lot, she said it really captured the essence of who I am. The next person to read it went ballistic. Her fears came flying out as she screamed, "how are you going to get known?" followed by, "how are you going to market yourself?" and "why can't you just stick to normal ways and just get a job?"

Good questions I suppose. But you know what? The universe didn't want me to get a job like everyone else. God knows I've tried every which way to fit in and be normal and be like everyone else. But my path was elsewhere. I just didn't have the confidence to pursue that path then. I had no idea how to market myself and go be a consultant. My current view is that my job is to write books about it and seed the thoughts and give you the tools to do the work yourself. As one psychic friend put it, "you can reach many more people with your writing than you can by doing individual and group consulting or therapy." She is absolutely right. When I write I have time to pull my thoughts together. After the books are written it may be time to go teach seminars based on the material in them. Or not.

New ideas often scare people. What happened when I got screamed at? Well, I felt squashed, for one. The person doing the screaming was projecting her fears onto me. She hadn't allowed herself to take risks and pursue what she really wanted to do. She too had had her dreams squashed as unrealistic and not allowed. So she was being human and passing on her projections. Imagine if we could recognize the issues when they come flying out. She could have taken her fears into therapy instead of dumping them on me. I could have taken my feelings of not being supported and understood into therapy and found the confidence to follow my true path. Instead I've taken the long road around but in the end I'll get there.

Eight

Discover your theme

Now let's talk about how you can go about discovering your own thread or theme. There are lots of ways to get there. When you read these instructions, you may come up with an even better idea. I think that's wonderful and part of the intent of this book. To get you, the reader, so involved that your creative juices start flowing and you build upon what I share here.

To discover my re-engineering thread I pulled out all my work records, and more. Performance reviews, job descriptions, projects I'd been involved in at work, home and for fun. I pulled out studies, courses, hobby activities, organizations I had belonged to and functions I had filled. I even went back to childhood to look at what activities had been my favorites then.

Perhaps this is the most daunting part. To pull together your experiences into one big pile before you start sorting. The effort will be worth it, so hang in there, practice some perseverance. And remember you don't have to do this in one go. You could designate a place, like a box or table, where you put all the stuff you find related to your thread search. Look at it like a treasure hunt and it becomes easier. For some of you it may make more sense to write it down as you think of it, in a notebook or on pieces of scrap paper. I use the scrap paper method a lot for my writing. I jot down an idea on a piece of paper, put it in a pile and then pull it out when I'm ready to write. That's when I sort through it, digging for inspiration and ideas.

"Now what?" you ask. "I've collected this huge pile of information but I haven't a clue how to make sense of it." Well, here's how I deal with it. For me, it seems to be trial and error. I sort things one way, then I look at it from a different angle. I let it rest for awhile. I pick it up again, sort it a different way, discard what doesn't fit or seem essential and go at it again. It becomes an iterative process. The resting phases in between seem essential for the honing into wonderful aha's.

The important thing is to start, and to keep at it over time so you complete the process. As a first step, simply read through everything you've collected. Notice how you felt about each accomplishment or activity. Take all the ones you feel really good about and put them in a special pile. It doesn't matter what anyone else thinks, this is your life, not your husband's or your Mom's or your friend's. What matters is finding the stuff that makes you glow.

Which activities give you the most satisfaction? This does not have to be work related, or make sense. If your joy is baking cookies, fishing, repairing cars, listening to stories in a bar, sex, telling others what to do, or not having to think, then write that down. Collect all the satisfaction activities and projects into one pile and work on that. If you feel ambitious you can go through your entire pile and note satisfaction threads. For most people that is simply too daunting, so just pull out the major happy stuff.

If you think about it, there are times when life just seems to click, or float. We do without effort, what we're doing feels so natural that we lose track of time. Some people describe it as, "easy as falling off a log." When people express amazement at, "how do you do that?" pay attention. Often our answer is, "oh that's nothing" because it truly isn't an effort. What you are looking for are those things that you do as easy as falling off a log, that you enjoy and are no effort for you. You are looking for your natural gifts and talents.

Perhaps your skill is being a good listener? Perhaps you have a knack for solving problems? Perhaps you are really good with details and repetitive chores? Perhaps your talent is cooking? Perhaps you love cleaning house? Perhaps you enjoy solitude, or the opposite, having lots of people and noise around you?

Myers-Briggs

One of my favorite personality tests is the Myers-Briggs indicator. It helps you understand your need for solitude versus people interaction, your comfort level with facts versus intuition, whether you base your decisions on thoughts or feelings and how you deal with time structure and open-ended flow in your life. I highly recommend this test to anyone.

The first time I took the test, was soon after I left the corporate world. I tested INTJ. When I retook the test a few years ago, I had shifted to an INFP. So what do these letters stand for?

The first letter is either **I** for *Introvert* or **E** for *Extrovert* and has to do with how we recharge our batteries. An introvert uses solitary activities to relax and needs undisturbed time alone to find new inspiration. An extrovert gets energized by being around other people and finds inspiration by bouncing ideas off other people.

The second letter is either **N** for *iNtuitive* or **S** for *Sensing*. Someone who is good with details and facts is a sensor. The intuitive deals in visions and dreams and will make decisions without knowing all the facts. Sensors will tell us intuitives we "wing it" or "fly by the seat of our pants."

The third letter is either **F** for *Feeling* or **T** for *Thinking*. A feeler makes decisions based on how they feel about something, whereas a thinker will think it through, it has to make logical sense to them. Another way to look at it, the feeler decides with his heart and the thinker decides with her head.

The fourth letter is either **J** for *Judgment* or **P** for *Perceiving*. The judger tends to be goal focused and does not easily get sidetracked. The perceiver can set out on a goal, but on the way stops to smell the roses, and loses sight of the goal. The judger likes closure and definite plans, whereas the perceiver needs a more open-ended approach to life. At the extreme ends the perceiver is into flow and the judger into structure.

If you know your MBTI profile, great! If not you may want to check it out. There are lots of really good books on the subject. I feel the MBTI has more to do with how we go about doing whatever we do, than the actual what we do. In other words, many professions can be practiced by several of the types, but each type would go about it in a different way and be most valuable, and happy, in a role where they could put their type to use.

Where is your passion?

Whether or not you've got your MBTI, you can continue the exercise to find your thread. Mentally go back through your life and remember each time you lost track of time and space. Focus on these activities. Write down what appears to be common denominators. What occurs in your life over and over? Look for repetition or similarities. Is there a uniqueness that you add to whatever you're doing?.

You may not get a definitive description of what it is, but you will start to get a sense. Ask your Higher Self to show you what your unique gifts are to the world. Remember that our logical brains often take us on side roads. It wants to be practical and will push aside the more imaginative ideas that pop up. Telling the logical brain to, "give it a rest" is sometimes appropriate!

In our life mission group, there was an artist who made a particular type of painting, which had been a commercial success. As he talked, his imagination mind would seed new ideas. His face would become animated and his gestures more alive as he explored other creative ideas. Then his logical mind would come in and remind him of the commercial success of his formula paintings and you could see the life energy disappear from his face.

To pay attention to life energy come alive or go dead is not something we normally think about. The shifts can be very quick and very subtle. We're not trained to follow this life energy. We are trained to squash natural impulses. We are trained to be practical, to get good jobs, to make money, to be responsible. We're not taught how to live.

To discover your essence or thread of what you really do best, you are looking for that which makes you come alive. It's where your essence comes through. It's where someone could stand you up in a corner and you just keep talking because you are so excited about it.

My brother, when he came home from Marine Corps boot camp, talked non-stop about his experience. It was the most alive and happy I've ever seen him. He was really in his essence, he was so excited, and not surprisingly he graduated at the top of his class. As a child, he read all the military type comic books and studied Morse code.

He also took radios apart and put them back together, with no parts left over! - a skill that really impresses me. As an adult he's rebuilt lasers, he's got a hands-on practical technical ability that is quite special. When we were children, he learned how to wait tables and be of service. He has a knack for languages and is quite social. He wanted to be an airline purser, but he was too tall for the standards then. His MBTI type is ENFJ. Translated he is an extrovert, intuitive, feeler and judger.

A good way to discover your essence is to look at your passion. Is your passion to help people heal? as it is for one of my therapy colleagues. She will stop at nothing if she can help you heal. No matter the time nor place, she will put her hands on you to help you heal. That's her passion.

At a dinner recently, I watched a woman come alive as she described what she does. "I'm a pre-school teacher. I love teaching and helping form the children." You could literally see her heart warm and the glow on her face as she talked about the children.

Seeing the essence or life energy in a persons face is the same process therapists use to catch unresolved emotions and issues. But instead of probing for pain, you probe for pleasure. The observation techniques are the same, just a different thread. Why not get together with one or more people to do this exercise? Simply watch and look for excitement. Observe expression come alive or go dead as the conversation meanders. Make sure to have as a ground rule to suspend logical practical thinking and just let yourselves play. Become fearless explorers of your own passions.

Nine

From theory to practice

It may be helpful at this point to go through in some detail what I actually did in the re-engineering examples I cited earlier. How did we get from A to Z?

Eliminating reports

Eliminated 75% of reports previously generated that were found to be non-essential.

I had moved into a new position that combined three jobs into one. There was no way I could do everything that three people had done previously. That was the whole point of consolidating jobs - to streamline while learning to learn to perform only those tasks that were truly essential. It meant prioritizing. Over the years, a large number of reports had been added to the routine functions of my predecessors. If I were to continue all of them, that in itself would have been a full time job.

How do you discover which reports are truly essential? Not an easy task. Call everyone on the reception lists? Make a survey and collate the results? Negotiate changes and consolidations? I had hit the deck running with this job and was on a fast track learning curve. There wasn't exactly a lot of time to schmooze with all the report recipients.

One day the penny dropped, the light bulb went on. Simply quit sending out the reports. Then wait for people to ask for the information they truly need. Sure enough, it worked. Turned out most of the reports that were previously sent out were never missed. The information people actually used was about 25% of the previous total.

One by one, people would call, "what happened to such and such report that your predecessor sent out?" they would ask. "Oh, I wanted to see which reports were actually read and used," I replied, "so I quit sending them out. Now tell me, what information do you need to do your job? In what form, how often, what do you do with it?"

We'd talk, I would get the information I needed to restructure the reports to be truly useful. In working with the recipients in this way I also built relationships with them. I asked what the customer needed. And I simplified my job - a lot. Writing reports is not a money making activity in most businesses, but rather a tool for the organization to use in making that money. It's important to focus on that which gives the biggest bang for the buck. Being busy is not the same as being effective. And efficiency is not necessarily congruent with being in the flow of life energy. When we follow the life energy, we take what appears to be detours that actually lead us more effectively to where we need to go.

The next re-engineering example is perhaps a better one to illustrate life energy flow.

Connect the dots

Increased quality levels and streamlined communications by connecting users directly with producers at shop floor level.

I see organizations as a flow of life energy. It's very simple really. Organize the work around the natural flow of energy and your organization will work very well and make money for you. People will be happier and you eliminate unneeded bureaucracy.

In the old organization, if there was a problem with packaging supplies on the shop floor, the employee would need to contact his or her supervisor, who in turn contacted the quality control supervisor, who in turn contacted me as the person responsible for purchasing packaging materials. I would contact the sales manager at the supplier, he would contact their quality control manager, who would contact the production manager and in the end get to the employee who actually produced the stuff.

Many organizations have this system. You can imagine how diluted and delayed the information gets by the time it gets back to the guy who made it. It doesn't even make much sense, but that's true of many organization ideas. They are built on control and hierarchy and not on the natural flow of energy.

I started talking to the people in the whole communication chain. I said, "look, if we could connect the actual user directly with the producer, we would simplify the process and improve the communication chain. How about we look at ways to connect them and the rest of us step out of the chain?" I was lucky that I worked in a place and in an environment where new ideas were welcomed and the overall objective of the business was to drive decisions to the lowest possible level and streamline operations.

In my discussions with all the people involved we came up with a plan. Our shop floor personnel would visit the supplier's manufacturing plant and get to know the people and their process. Then the supplier's shop floor personnel would come to our factory. The project was a huge success. Not only were quality levels improved, but new production improvement ideas surfaced, relationships were built, processes understood and best of all, our shop floor employees were empowered.

More than once I heard, "if I have a problem with wrappers from our supplier, I just pick up the phone and call the guy who made them, and we sort it out between us." You could hear the pride in their voices. They liked feeling a part of the chain. The rest of us were superfluous to that process. We put in place a system where we would be informed on a summary basis, which served our needs. And yes, rejects went down and quality levels improved.

Getting the people involved, making them a part of the process and empowering them to make decisions that affect them, works every time. It's been said many times before by many different people, but it bears repeating.

Re-engineering a whole process

Reduced development cycle time 60% from concept to finished product by discovering real instead of written processes and procedures, by streamlining communication flows, by upgrading capability of people involved in the material flow chain, by learning the supplier manufacturing processes to understand what information they needed at what time and in what form. Sales volume went from zero to one million cases per year.

There is already a fair amount of description in the above statement. If you go back and review the seven steps of re-engineering you will find that all of them were used in the reduction of development cycle time. I did not do this all on my own. Many other people were part of the process. You can't create change in a vacuum, and this project nicely illustrates that organizations are relationships and vice versa.

The particular process involved here was new packaging development.

We were in a time of many changes. We were going after the warehouse club market. Instead of traditional case packs the vendor demanded palletized loads that displayed well and could be put directly into the store. That demanded a big rethink on our part, not only from a manufacturing point of view but also from our suppliers of packaging material as well as our whole logistics operation.

I will stick to the warehouse club process as it applies to all the packaging development processes.

First step was to **learn** about the warehouse club way of doing business. We went on field trips to stores. We talked internally and with our suppliers. We'd kick ideas around. There were formal and informal meetings. When we started we didn't even have approval to create a new brand. It all started when some trial packs were made up at a contract packager, the local sales manager called on Costco, pitched the idea and got an order. Our procedural types at corporate headquarters had a fit, chewed us out for not following the established procedures, but truth is had we waited for them we never would have got the business. You have to be able to take risks in order to grow. As true in business as it is in your personal life.

Second step is called **build relationships**. In order to get anything done in the world, you have to have people connections. You can't live in a vacuum and you are dependent on other people to live and work. The better you can build your work relationships the easier it is to work with each other and get things done. The relationship building during this process was on-going. By embarking on a learning expedition you automatically start the relationship building. As you seek information you also interact with the other people.

Pay attention to how they think. How they function. If they need a lot of pre-planning and structure of if they fly more by the seat of their pants. This is one area where Myers Briggs type is useful. I wish we'd had it as a tool then. Astrology is another area I find fascinating and useful, more on this ahead.

Third step I call **brainstorm**. You can do this by yourself or with a group. You've gathered a lot of information and by now you know each other well enough to toss ideas around and be able to discuss them. I find that brainstorming works well as an iterative process. You generate ideas then go off and do something else. Come back and chew on them a bit, hatch some new ideas, discard some and make new combinations.

In brainstorming it is imperative to send the critical mind on vacation.

Absolutely no "Yeah, but..." allowed. Getting into a playful or meditative state before you start is good. Bringing in a facilitator for creative processes may be helpful as is going into a different environment. Shifting environment frees up energy as does doing things differently than we are used to.

After brainstorm comes **prioritize**. This is a first cut, you generally have many more ideas than you could possibly implement. Letting the visionaries have at it is useful at this stage, because they will see possibilities the bean counters never will. Why is this? Because a bean counter is detail oriented, here and now, sees what is and what has been but is not good at dreaming. The visionary however, is pretty useless at day-to-day details like bookkeeping, but excels at seeing possibilities. Most new products and ideas are pooh-poohed by the practical types. We live in different worlds.

If Henry Ford had been practical we would not have had his automobiles. He had a good paying steady job so why should he pursue this crazy dream? If Bill Gates had finished college and got his degree like a practical person he never would have started Microsoft. There are many examples where being practical will not fulfill your dreams. There is no value judgment here about visionary or practical types being better or worse than the other. We simply need to recognize that each one excels at different things.

When you prioritize you look at all the ideas and try to put them in order of most to least important or most to least interesting. Then pick one, two or maybe three at the top to focus on. This is another key to long range success. Focusing on a few key projects instead of trying to manage a whole lot gets you farther in the end. Not all projects have the same importance or long-term value.

Moving along in the re-engineering process we're now ready to **analyze**. Here the bean counters are very useful. See, each and every one of us has a very important job to do and each and every one of us is essential for the whole - from the person who does the janitorial service to the CEO of the company.

Each and every one of us is essential to the whole process. See it's Divinely planned that way. The key is to understand ourselves and each other well enough to know who would do what best. Learn to work with the life energy so that the structure and flow are optimized.

Of the ideas prioritized as most interesting there are a number of factors that can be analyzed. In the warehouse clubs process we analyzed potential sales and production figures, recalculated manufacturing costs, re-evaluated supplier and vital supplies processes. Each project is unique. There is something about going through nuts and bolts calculations that help to clarify the best alternatives. Life is part winging it and part dollars and cents.

It has to make "cents."

Now we get to the **plan and organize** step. Whenever you re-engineer an entire process you have to essentially go back to the beginning and start the planning process all over again. It's like when you're computerizing a whole process, for example material resource planning. You don't just take the existing process and dump it into the computer. No, you look at it as if you were to design the process today from scratch. Ask yourself, "what would the process look like today, if I utilized the tools available on the computer? What is the actual information flow? How is the product put together?"

The actual, or informal communication chain is seldom the same as the organization plan calls for. Whenever you can align the business with the de facto communication chain, you will benefit.

When you have learned about all the existing ways of doing things, when you have brainstormed new ideas and analyzed them, you can proceed to organize the whole shebang into a new whole. The key here is to let go of the way things have been done. Let yourself think outside the box.

In the warehouse club project the changes were gradual and iterative. We tested our way along, tried some ideas, discarded some, talked about it, and then continued the improvements. So the reduction in development cycle time evolved in due course. Your project is likely to be the same way - you won't go from 1 to 10 in one step, you will iterate and go through steps 2, 3, 4, 5, 6, 7, 8 and 9 on the way and not necessarily in that order. You may do 4 then 3 then back to 7 and so on but in the end you get there.

But remember it's a journey. If we could only keep that in mind when we get so focused on a goal that we lose sight of living here and now.

Last but not least we get to **implement** by putting all those ideas into practice. The new processes, the revised order system and the new contract packager brought on line.

One of the major contributions to our success was the involvement of everyone in the entire chain. We brought in our suppliers to be partners in the process. They came up with some innovative designs we couldn't have. We tapped the capabilities of the contract packagers. We sought their ideas and involvement. It really pays off to let people think and be creative and let them come up with their own ideas. The most stifling way to treat people is to walk in with a pre-determined solution that they are to implement. That's when you get in trouble, as there is no ownership from the very people you are dependent on to implement the new solution.

Participative management

Increased engineering staff productivity 10% by developing new planning model for prioritizing and assigning projects.

When I took over as engineering supervisor for the Paper Mill Engineering group we had about 120 projects on the wish list and six engineers to do all the work. We were responsible for both maintenance and capital projects so the scope of the 120 projects varied considerably, from a simple calculation or minor rerouting of piping to mini-rebuilds of the paper machines.

The projects would come to us as engineering requests, submitted by the production or maintenance departments. When I took over, there wasn't a system in place to effectively deal with long versus short term priorities or a way to decide which project should got done first. We were often in "fire fighting" mode, responding to the urgency of the day. Needless to say, the engineers got jerked around and seldom had the peace to focus on the long-range money making improvement projects.

It became clear to me we needed to do something. I suppose I had an advantage in that I was promoted from the group I was supervising. I knew the work well and all the players involved. They knew my capabilities and I had their respect.

I started chatting with the production and maintenance guys who were our customers. I explored with them the idea of designing some priority system so we could be more effective, where they would have a clearer idea of what projects we were actually working on. They were open to the idea of discussing it.

Good, step one, the customers are at least willing to listen to ideas. Without their buy-in it would have been senseless to do what I did next. I sat my engineers down and solicited their thoughts and feelings. Not surprisingly, they needed to ventilate their frustrations with the current system. The biggest gripe was too many projects assigned and not a clear priority when the urgency of the week appeared.

I asked them what a reasonable project load would be. How many projects were manageable at one time? As we talked back and forth and they pondered this type and that type and allowing for all the phases of a project they gradually came to the consensus that six projects was a reasonable load. If I were to do this today, I would probe for individual differences, someone may do well to carry more, others less or be suitable for particular types of jobs. But hey, it was my first experience as a supervisor. First woman ever in the job to boot.

The other problem we had, with recurring fire fighting issues, got resolved with the help of the maintenance planning engineer and supervisor. The three of us attended the production meetings and were the ones who internally had to sort out how to handle the latest emergency. We came up with a plan to first of all keep track of the fire fighting projects. We then agreed that those that recurred we would assign as projects to be stayed on and kept at until solved at their core. So many recurring problems are never solved at their core. Until they are, they just keep popping back up, like a jack-in-the-box, over and over. Countless hours are wasted chasing your tail. Usually, some other urgent business comes up, this one isn't acting up at the moment, so it is dropped, the engineer is sent off on another goose chase until it crops back up again. A never ending merry-go-round.

So we resolved to keep someone on it until the root problem was solved. We also agreed that when asked to pick up another hot item we would patiently ask, "which project do we drop in order to start this one? Is this one more important than a, b or c?"

I had a monthly engineering meeting that all our customers attended. I went through all our projects, reviewed current status and issued a summary report. When we introduced the new system the first order of business for me was prioritizing all the projects and explaining our new guidelines. We would have a limit of six projects per engineer and resolve fire fighting issues at the core. I also started a new category of projects "ready to install." Here I put projects that were not actively being worked on but would demand the engineer's entire attention when that production unit would be shut down for maintenance.

We went through some start-up pains but the engineers loved having the peace to focus on fewer projects and less starts and stops. The resolution of long standing fire fighting problems did take some time. We had problems that recurred sure as clockwork and had for years. Now we just didn't give up until we figured out the real cause.

One heater problem turned out to be caused by the supplier having shipped the wrong unit. The one installed was undersized for the job it needed to do. The detective work to uncover that one took a long time but it sure was worth it in the end. That's usually the key to recurring problems, you have to put on your detective cap and stay at digging for and analyzing clues until you catch the real culprit.

Our productivity went up, my estimate is that we accomplished 10% more with the new planning model. Job satisfaction went way up for the engineers. In time, our customers were happier too, with less recurring problems and a clear system to deal with priorities.

Not bad for a first crack at supervision - by a girl to boot. My my.

Ten

Pentacle of M

Maybe this is an appropriate time to introduce some other ideas I put together while I was pondering my existence and reason for being. When I was job hunting and writing resumes I was searching for a deeper sense of what I was about. To me, there was a need to express the *why* I did things. To discover my underlying values. To define what I thought I brought to the world. I love playing with words and I love it when the letters roll nicely off the tongue, as in *Meandering Mind*. It feels synergistic.

After much pondering and sorting I came up with the *Pentacle of M*:

Money "The Management of Wealth made Simple"

Motto "Everything has Room for Improvement"

Method "Cooperation and Mutual Support"

Motivation "The Quest for Knowledge"

Mission "To be a Catalyst for Change"

You know, it still fits. I believe our relationships to *money* should be easy, that financial systems and controls are best when simple. My *motto* describes my attitude toward life, there is always a way to improve on what has been done before. There's always a better mousetrap to be found.

The best *method* to use in networks and organizations is to scratch each other's backs. When we cooperate with each other the work flows smoothly and helping each other multiplies the results. Mary Kay expressed it so well, "if I have an idea and you have an idea and we share our ideas with each other, then we both have two ideas." Her revolutionary ideas of how to run a business paid off as Mary Kay became the number one cosmetics company in the United States. More on her in a bit.

Understanding your *motivation*, what drives you, can help you understand how to make a job exciting. I really am on a quest for knowledge, so any undertaking has to include learning for me to be happy. The more we can understand our MO the better we can be at doing what we do. I'm pitiful in jobs where it's all laid out and all there is left to do is execute. Boring. To someone else that is a dream. They don't have to figure it out, they can just sit down and get to work. We are all different.

Then last, but certainly not least, is my *mission*, to be a catalyst for change. Actually, I would like to see much more of this type of thinking around career planning and job searches. We need help early on in sorting out "who am I?" and "how do I fit?" The pentacle of M can be applied to relationships and organizations and next we'll do some exercises around this.

These exercises are suitable for everyone, whether you are in a relationship, an organization or on your own. They will help you clarify your underlying values in a new way. Play with the different exercises and feel free to change them as you see fit. Share them with others and dialogue about your discoveries. Go back and review the talking dog exercise and use it to dialogue. I have repeated my M's for reference.

Money "The Management of Wealth made Simple"

Money is one of those loaded subjects that can get the emotions flying. Conflicting values about money is one of the biggest stressors in relationships. If you can dialogue about your differences and discover how to arrange your affairs to minimize conflict, wouldn't it be worth doing? But first you have to get clear on what your own beliefs are.

If you had an unlimited supply of money, what would you do with it? Take this question and write about it, dialogue about it and explore your fears, hopes and beliefs as you do this. Be honest with yourself and explore your feelings and thoughts about money. Are there any beliefs you'd like to change?

Keep digging beyond the surface stuff, do the exercise several times. Pay attention to what comes in the second or third go around. This is where we tuck the real treasures, the values that actually drive us. It's so important to dig beneath the surface, because what our conscious mind says is not the driver, it's the subconscious that is in charge. When we can discover what is in our subconscious, we can align ourselves with our true values and beliefs. If we don't like what comes up we can change our beliefs.

One more exercise to access your core values and beliefs about money. *Brainstorm.* What thoughts, words or images pop up in your awareness around money? Just keep repeating the mantra money, money, money, money, money... catch the thought. Repeat the mantra money, money, money, money, money... see the picture. Repeat the mantra money, money, money, money, money... hear the sound. Repeat the mantra money, money, money, money, money... and savor its taste. Repeat the mantra money, money, money, money, money... and inhale the smell. Could it be the sweet smell of success?

Motto "Everything has Room for Improvement"

How do you come up with a **motto**? I don't think it's necessary to come up with a punchy statement unless you get your kicks from it like I do. But exploring themes and which mottos appeal to you can be a fun exercise and help you learn something about yourself.

For fun, get on the internet and do a motto search. My current favorite search engine is Google. By the time you read this there may be something even better out there. Engage your family, friends and colleagues and go on a motto hunt. Collect as many mottos as you can find, make a list and print it out.

Then cut the paper so each motto is on a separate piece of paper. Put the scraps into a jar or bowl, then draw them out one by one. For the motto you have pulled out, try to describe the type of person this represents, what they are like and what they stand for.

Or, take the list and circle the mottos that appeal to you then work on refining them until you come up with your own.

Method "Cooperation and Mutual Support"

To discover how you go about doing what you do, you may want to play journalist for a bit. Go interview people you know, it doesn't matter if they are social acquaintances or people you've worked with for years. Ask them to tell you how they perceive you, how they would describe your **method** for coping with the world. You may gain some valuable insights and find some surprises too. Remember that we see through different lenses, and although we are all looking at the same elephant, to use a common metaphor, one of us has the ears as a focus, another the trunk, another the legs and so on. So when we describe the elephant from one viewpoint it may not sound like it's the same animal when we hear it described from another's viewpoint.

Motivation "The Quest for Knowledge"

What **motivates** you? I think this is best done as an inner exercise. There is always a thread or two through everything we do. I've discovered that learning is the key for me. To discover, to think new thoughts and to combine ideas in new ways excites me. For you it may be helping others, or being accurate, or responsible and so on. Sometimes the answer pops up immediately and you are clear as a bell on your inner motivation. Other times you have to work harder to see the thread. Don't worry, the insights you really need will come to you when you truly need them. It is human to want to know now and be impatient, however our spiritual lesson is to learn to trust. Sigh, such a hard lesson for some of us to learn as that impatient kid inside bounces up and down demanding to know now!

Mission "To be a Catalyst for Change"

Understanding our **mission** is a key piece. My job is to be a catalyst. I'm not here to take you through years of training or to provide all the answers. I'm here to stir the pot, to plant new seeds.

There have been entire books written on the subject of life mission, so to expect a simple exercise to cover it all won't do. But I can get you started and perhaps my exercise will give you what you need for now. If you want to dig deeper there's lots more material out there.

So how do you figure out your mission, the why you are here? And while we are on the subject, there are many ways and several statements that can cover your mission. I also have as a mission to change the role of women on the planet. I do this simply by being myself. But it could also entail political engagement. The how you carry it out can vary a lot.

What is a life mission? Remember the religious notion of a calling, a vocation? This is far beyond a job. Each person on this earth is here for a specific reason.

Janene Jurgensen, whose life mission was to help other people find their life mission, wrote:

"A true life mission is life/work that is in perfect harmony with all levels of one's being and in alignment with the good of the whole. It will stimulate, excite, challenge, stretch and support. It will not compromise values, jeopardize health or stress emotions.

There are many levels to our being. These are sometimes referred to as bodies. Our causal body (also sometimes called the memory body) holds detailed records of our previous incarnations. It also contains a matrix related to one's life mission. The Life Mission Matrix is derived from past life records. It is an exact accounting of how one can balance the accumulation of karmic debt through doing specific service, their life mission.

The Life Mission Matrix is located in the Causal Body at the solar plexus chakra or Will Center. Alignment with this matrix requires attunement with the whole or with Divine Will. When one is aligned and resonating with the Life Mission Matrix each atom, molecule and cell in the lower bodies is charged with the vibration of the mission."

Your life mission is a main driver in anything you do. One therapy colleague stops at nothing to help people heal. Another leaves no stone unturned when she works on you. Some of my other therapy colleagues have missions that focus on teaching, on developing training material and course structure. A mission is always tied in with what excites you about life and your work. Ok you say, "this is all very interesting, but where is the exercise you promised on life mission?" You need wait no longer, for here it is:

In a way it's simple and yet it is not. The exercise is to pray and then wait for the answer. *My life mission is now revealed to me by the Divine Source* is the only statement you need to make. Do adapt the prayer to fit your beliefs and religion and rituals. Then know in your heart that you will be answered. The answer may come soon or it may come after a long wait. It may come as a vague sense or clear as a bell. It may come symbolically in a dream or as a statement in your head. You may doubt it when it comes. If you do, ask to talk to your Higher Self, just to make sure you are connected to the Source and not just any astral entity.

Eleven

Life Mission Group

Maybe now would be a good time to talk about the Life Mission group I was a part of. We shared a common interest in understanding what life mission was all about and how to find our own path in life. We'd bring brown bag lunches and meet for a few hours every other week.

Just getting together and sharing thoughts and ideas started the ball rolling. Several in the group had felt they were not where they were supposed to be and sure enough, the universe made it clear to them.

One woman fell on the way to work. Then when she got there, the computer system crashed and the phone system shut down. A pretty clear message that she was in the wrong place.

Another woman had gotten a traffic ticket for not following signs. She confirmed that she wasn't following the signs in her life for the direction she really wanted and needed to go.

Another woman woke up one morning and heard, "your mission is to help other people find their life mission." Appropriately enough, she was the first facilitator of our group.

Just getting together and talking, sharing and doing exercises helped move us along. We explored personality tests, read books, bounced ideas off each other and supported each other emotionally. We were exploring territory that was pretty new then. If you feel like starting a life mission group of your own, there are many exercises in my books that are suitable.

Spa Healing Temple

Another project formed about the same time as the Life Mission group, but with a slightly different people make-up. Called The Spa Healing

Temple, it was a vision for a whole new way to approach healing, nurturing and spirituality.

The founding members of the Life Mission group and Spa Healing Temple project have since passed over to the other side. They helped seed the energy structure and are now available as support from the other side to a larger group of people.

A *Spa Healing Temple* could be cabins in the woods, a downtown spa or any center where healing, spirituality and pleasure are key ingredients. It could have any name. Spa Healing Temple is a concept, not a franchise idea. It may be a center with a bookstore, café or restaurant, treatment rooms for therapy, large classroom space as well as meditation room.

Many in the new age community have tried to build a center or school only to walk away frustrated over the power struggles that invariably ensue. Therapy organizations are no different, it's amazing how often people get caught in petty politics of who gets authorized to teach, or is included or excluded, accepted or not. Until we heal enough so we can open the door to show others our vulnerability and get out of power-over and into empowerment none of these organizations will work. What I do know is that any project of this type would need to be built on a foundation of regular group meditation and with members who are doing their own inner work. Otherwise the egos just take off and create havoc.

I love the writing of Florence Scovel Shinn and Emmet Fox. They explain so eloquently the principle of: that which belongs to us by Divine right, or by right of consciousness, is ours, we cannot lose it. It is guaranteed that we have it. We may not get what we think we want, but we always get what we need, when the time is right.

We need to work from a basis of inner wisdom where each and every one of us is connected to and gets directed by the Higher Self. Where we operate from Spiritual principles and really own that what is mine by right of consciousness can't be taken from me and really understand that to try to occupy the space that belongs to another is a violation of Spiritual law. We need to learn to surrender to the higher wisdom. Part of that is to let go of the abdication of power to a guru, leader or another human. We need to be willing to send the ego on a long hike on a short pier. Isn't it time to let petty squabbles go? Bickering about what is included in this theory or teaching, or rules about certification and all those other obstacles to the free flow of energy, information and knowledge have no place in the organizations of the future. A free flowing discussion of ideas by all means, but please no more thought police!

When we teach or heal or do whatever it is we do, it needs to come from real life experience, where you know it in every cell of your body and not just your head. If your base belief is that there isn't enough in the world to go around, that if another wins you lose, then the new organization model won't work for you. To make organizations of the future work they have to be based on a belief that there is more than enough for everyone, that there is no limit to love or money or what is possible. If you are coming from fear and think that you have to take from others to win, if you believe in competition instead of cooperation then the new organization models aren't going to work for you.

All humans, including healers and teachers are *unfinished* or *works in process* or *wounded*. It's how we work through our issues when they surface that determines the outcome. We need to balance working on others and working on ourselves. It's easy to fall into the trap that you know more than others and that you have the answers to their problems. The other side of that trap is when we put others on a pedestal. I've encountered several leaders in the alternative health movement who are more unhealed than the people they are trying to heal, and who seem unable to let go of control.

One of the exercises we did in the life mission group clarified for me that I have a special skill in helping people get from here to there. Symbolically, a colleague saw me standing at the shore of a body of water, with fog obscuring the visibility so you couldn't see across to the other shore. Most people would see only the fog, but not the other side. He said, "you see through the fog to the other side. You see how to build the bridge across, where the rest of us see fog." Hmm, I thought, this is very interesting. What can I do with this?

I was still in the mode of wanting to apply my skills in a larger context, finding work somehow. So I wrote an abstract:

Transition Management – building a bridge to tomorrow

Inherent in every organization is the potential of what could be. As yet unrealized possibilities. Glimmers of a dream. A memory of what you came here to accomplish. A whisper of an idea, which if allowed to grow, could dramatically alter the achievements of your organization.

Imagine you are a group of people with an idea, some dream you want to manifest, some discovery you want to make, and some product you want to develop. How do you manifest that dream, how do you take it from the idea stage to reality, how do you build that bridge to tomorrow?

The answer is Transition Management. There is a unique skill in being able to stand at the shore and see how to create that bridge to the other side. A Transition Manager works with a group of people wanting to create "tomorrow." The Transition Manager guides and facilitates the process by becoming part of the group for the duration of the project.

Perhaps the most important piece to Transition Management is to get clear on what the group is hoping to accomplish. Where are we going and why? What is our purpose, vision and mission? What is the essence of what we are trying to accomplish? What is at the core, what is it that drives our passion, what is our raison d'être?

As part of this process it is essential to get the clutter out of the way, so we can really tap into the core. In other words, we need to clear the fog. How can we build a bridge to tomorrow, if we can't see the shore on the other side?

It is at this point we start to put our thoughts on paper, perhaps via questionnaires, perhaps by making sketches, collages or models, or perhaps by writing essays answering the question: if there were no limits, what would our project look like?

From this tangible representation of the group consciousness, a Transition Manager can lay out the critical path to success. Now it becomes possible to develop the strategic plan and be clear on how to take the next step. It is the start of building the bridge to tomorrow.

As we move into the implementation phase, staying focused on priorities becomes essential. For each step we take, we review our progress, alter our course as necessary, and learn along the way. At the completion of the project, the Transition Manager leaves the team for another assignment.

Client Comments:

"her in-depth technical know-how combined with a multi-language capability made her a very valuable member of the project management team"

"has a strong business focus and makes sound and timely decisions"

"has the ability to get to the heart of a problem"

"a willing listener...considerate of others viewpoints...a pleasure to work with"

"extremely well organized and very efficient at prioritizing"

"excellent delegator with a strong emphasis on personal growth" "helps people move through transition"

"a self starter developing systems and methods to increase efficiency and organization"

"you get focus, direction and a push for your fledgling flight"

change is a creative process

The transition process described above could be used at the start-up of a company, a project or as an improvement process in an existing organization. Let the thoughts introduced above percolate in your consciousness for a while. In the meantime I want to talk about another organization with a very different approach to people building.

Twelve

Building people up

If you live outside the United States, you may not have heard of the most successful cosmetics company in America. Founder Mary Kay had worked in sales in a traditional company. She was very successful in this male dominated trade, but had her own ideas of how to build an even better organization. When she started her company, most thought she would fail with her crazy ideas. But it turned out she was right. There was a different way to run a successful business, especially if your sales force was made up of predominantly women. Little did she know when she started Mary Kay in Dallas, Texas that it would grow to be number one.

Mary Kay built what I call a *people building organization*. The guiding priorities for all employees and consultants at Mary Kay are:

God first

Relationships second

Career third

That's sure a different priority list! You may wonder how you can run a company on those premises. Sounds backwards, doesn't it? Actually, it makes more sense than any other priority system I've encountered. Let's take a look at each priority in turn.

God first means you tune into your spiritual guidance first. You let Spirit, or God, or Allah or your guru guide you. It doesn't matter if you pray, meditate or lay Tarot to get your guidance, they key principle is that you let Spirit, intuition and inspiration guide you.

Relationships second. In the Mary Kay write-ups it actually says family second, which I have chosen to alter to relationships second. What is meant here are our key, or most precious relationships, whether it be spouse, pet, close friend, children, or other significant people in our lives. It places a value and priority on the personal life, which many corporations miss.

Career third means that after we have tuned into God, after we have made space in our lives for key relationships, only then can we fully focus on our careers.

The sales force is made up of independent beauty consultants who sell via in-home classes. There are no territories, each consultant is under the guidance of a director. If the director who signed you up lives in a different area than you do, you go to the meetings of a director close to you. You get adopted by the local director who takes as much pride and care in helping you succeed as her own flock. There are weekly sales meetings where you gradually get trained to stand up and present in front of a group.

The Mary Kay system of gradually supporting and encouraging public speaking skills produces some of the best motivational speakers you'll find anywhere.

As the majority of the sales force is made up of women, the rewards are not only financial, but include lots of glitz and glamour, visible rewards like jewelry, clothes and pink Cadillac cars for the directors. The annual sales convention is definitely a dress up affair with tiaras and lots of glitter.

The symbol used in Mary Kay is the bumblebee. Aerodynamically it shouldn't be able to fly, but it does anyway. It is used as a reminder that anything is possible. It goes against what is commonly accepted to be true.

To assist the sales force in keeping their priorities straight, there is a system whereby you can ask a sister to do a class for you if, for example, your special someone surprises you with a dinner invitation. Furthermore, there is a ground rule that you don't steal customers from each other. If you run across someone who already buys from a sister, you say wonderful, you just keep buying from her. You never recruit from existing customers, that's a corporate no-no.

When I joined the Mary Kay Cosmetics organization I received the following letter printed on paper with a lovely red rose on it:

"And the day came when the risk to remain closed as a bud became more painful than the risk it took to blossom.

Like the covenant of the rainbow, the rose has become a symbol in MARY KAY of faith, love and caring humanity.

It's COLOR represents a positive quality of the giver.

It's VELVETY TEXTURE represents the quality of the receiver.

The GREEN LEAVES represents the growth of personal inner potential.

The THORNS represents challenges and obstacles to overcome.

The STEM represents the strength to remain constant in the pursuit of high ideals.

It's SCENT - why, of course! It's the sweet smell of SUCCESS!"

I wanted to include it here as it captures the essence of the whole Mary Kay organization. I felt so welcomed and supported the year I spent as an independent beauty consultant. In hindsight, I realize the main reason I joined the organization was to be exposed to a very different way of building people and organizations.

Sink or swim

It was so different from my earlier experience. Scott Paper was a great company in many ways, but their approach to building people was what I call the *sink or swim* method. What method? Yes, I call it sink or swim. What I mean is that you were given a project or task, then given free reins to go do it. If you needed help or had questions, it was up to you to go find someone who could help you.

So in a way you had a chance to take great risks and grow in the process. But it was very much like being thrown into the pond. Wonderful if you figured out how to swim. If you didn't you sank.

The difference between Scott Paper and Mary Kay was significant. At Scott Paper you could be given assignments you didn't feel ready for but you had to figure out how to do them anyway. At Mary Kay you were gradually groomed for the next challenge so each step didn't feel that daunting. And you got lots of support on the way. Perhaps the two approaches are indicative of the difference between traditional male and female thinking.

Thirteen

Relationships and astrology

I am a great fan of different personality tests and other indicators of personality. One such system is astrology. The deeper I study it, the more useful I find it. Nowadays the computer software to calculate charts and do comparisons is readily available and reasonably priced, even for the home user.

I found a great program called *Time Passages* by Henry Seltzer. The program is available for both Mac and PC users. My version also calculates what is known as *synastry*. Another new word. Synastry is astrology-speak for relationships. It compares the charts between two people to look at how the planets interact and predict where there will be tensions and difficulties and where there will be smooth sailing and support. The synastry calculations can be done for romantic relationships or for business/friendship relationships. Synastry can be quite useful for two people who deal with each other a lot.

Henry Seltzer publishes articles and monthly astrology updates on his website www.astrograph.com. I find his writing interesting and quite useful.

A more basic approach for astrology comes from a book by Linda Goodman called *Star Signs*. She put together a very brief career guide based on the sun signs. She called it the *Labor of Love*:

Labors of Love

LEADERS OF THOUGHT AND ACTION

| ARIES | March 20 - April 20 | Fire |
| CANCER | June 21 - July 22 | Water |

| LIBRA | September 23 - October 23 | Air |
| CAPRICORN | December 21 - January 20 | Earth |

ORGANIZERS OF THOUGHT AND ACTION

TAURUS	April 20 - May 21	Earth
LEO	July 22 - August 23	Fire
SCORPIO	October 23 - November 22	Water
AQUARIUS	January 20 - February 19	Air

COMMUNICATORS OF THOUGHT AND ACTION

GEMINI	May 21 - June 21	Air
VIRGO	August 23 - September 23	Earth
SAGITTARIUS	November 22 - December 21	Fire
PISCES	February 19 - March 20	Water

Fire signs labor with love in professions that are exciting, original, daring, inspiring, challenging, capable of arousing instant enthusiasm and provides an opportunity to express idealism.

Water signs labor with love in professions that are absorbing, deep, constantly moving, silently progressing, flexible and have an aura of mystery to stir the floods of imagination.

Air signs labor with love in professions that are unpredictable, unorthodox, unexpected, changing, lets them keep moving mentally and challenges their sharp intellects.

Earth signs labor with love in professions that are solid, stable, practical, well planned, well paid, have a firm foundation with strong and powerful growth potential.

At least when I read it I had a big aha. I'm a Sagittarian, so I am meant to labor with love in a profession that is exciting, original, daring, inspiring, challenging, capable of arousing instant enthusiasm and provides an opportunity to express idealism through communicating thought and action. Being a writer of this kind of book satisfies all of that. How well do Linda Goodman's descriptions fit your idea of what you love to do?

Fourteen

Someone to practice on

One of my friends who has experienced ups and downs with relationships told God that if she was to learn how to be in a relationship she needed someone to practice on. She said "how do you expect me to work through my issues if I don't have someone to practice on?" Very good question.

I've had a number of relationships where there seemed to be mutual interest, but we interacted so seldom, that when we would meet the sexual tensions were so charged, that it was hard to focus on anything else. I wish we could have spent more time talking and getting to know one another. Really talking.

A male colleague I worked with who was away from his family for extended periods on construction jobs looked at it another way. His boys would tell him that even though he was home much less than the fathers of their friends, they actually got to spend more time with their Dad, and it was fun quality time, to use an overused expression. They would go sailing or skiing when Dad was home, really taking advantage of the family being together. Maybe it is true that absence makes the heart grow fonder.

It is true that we tend to forget or not appreciate what we have if we get used to having it all the time. Maybe this is why Swedes are so obsessed with the weather, the seasons are short and intense, from very dark and cold in the winter to almost endless summer nights for a brief spell. That's when we all rush outside and soak up the sun and light so we can manage the long winters in hibernation when you may not see your neighbor for days.

Communication is key

So many relationships don't get off the ground because we don't know how to communicate with each other. Lest you think I have all the answers, I don't. What I can tell you are my observations of where we may be going wrong, and my thoughts on how to improve from there. Learning to communicate is so important, yet we spend essentially no time learning it.

How many of us were brought up in homes where our parents were skilled in resolving conflict? How many of us lived in homes where the interfamily communication was open and supportive? Our parents couldn't teach us what they didn't know how to do themselves. But if we stop and think about it we can discover new ways.

I suppose the most important is the communication we have with ourselves. I'm a firm believer in meditation as a way to connect with my inner self. It is here we explore what is within us, what is really percolating beneath the surface and can get hold of our deepest needs. I believe that to truly be able to communicate with another I need to know myself first.

Know thyself meditation

Therefore, I am going to introduce a meditation technique that is easy to learn and easy to practice. You can do this anywhere and anytime. There are no special tools needed and it doesn't matter if you are in a crowded airport or alone on a mountaintop – this technique works.

I find this easiest to do sitting down, preferably in a chair where you can feel your feet resting on the floor and you can sit with your spine straight. Begin by closing your eyes and taking a few deep breaths. Let your focus go inward, into your body and your senses. If there is noise around you, let that noise help you relax deeper and deeper into yourself. With practice you will get better at keeping your focus on you. It's normal in the beginning to hear every noise around you. With practice, you will still notice the noise, but it won't bother you nor distract you, it will simply be there.

Continue to breathe slowly and deeply. Let your awareness drift inward, become aware of your body, your thoughts, your emotions and your senses. Notice what you are aware of, just be present to whatever is going on within you. If you just had lunch and your stomach is making itself heard, be with your stomach. If you've just had a phone call from your sweetie and you are feeling euphoric, be with that sensation.

Whatever thought, whatever feeling, whatever sensation, simply place your awareness on that and let yourself go deeper into whatever your inner self brings up.

If the euphoria shifts to thoughts spinning around in your head, just let it happen. Notice what happens to your breathing as you sit quietly. Notice if your body speaks to you. Perhaps you all of a sudden notice your toe, or your nose itches. Keep your awareness on whatever comes up, there is nothing here to judge, there is nothing here to achieve, there is no goal or accomplishment to be reached. You are simply spending time with yourself and connecting to your inner self.

When I started meditating I used a timer. I made myself sit, just sit, for five minutes. I had come out of a very busy and stressful time in my life and to sit doing nothing for five minutes was a challenge. That was a long time ago. Now I can easily sit staring into space. I think we've lost the fine art of staring into space, simply being.

When you start this exercise, I recommend you do it five minutes per day. Finding five minutes in a day is easy and doable, there is no excuse in the world that can justify not having five minutes a day for yourself. Once you find five minutes doable and comfortable, extend it to ten, do that for awhile, then increase it to fifteen minutes a day. When you've reached a comfort level with fifteen minutes per day go ahead and increase it to twenty minutes. Then keep doing a twenty-minute meditation every day for the rest of your life. You will gradually notice a benefit. The real shift comes after three years of daily meditation or about a thousand days, then there's a shift in your brain and your consciousness.

Non-verbal communication

We tend to think of communication as verbal, as speaking or writing. But we send and receive messages in so many other ways. We are becoming a much more visually oriented society, where images flash across the screen conveying a whole message in a few seconds. We can say a lot with our eyes and facial expression as well as with our body language. Our tone of voice says a lot about how we really feel.

Touch is an underrated mode of communication. Our bodies love to touch and be touched. We talk about being touched emotionally by a song or a movie. But how often do we talk about being touched physically in the same way? We tend to think of physical touch as sexual. But it need not be. A massage is very satisfying for the body and is only rarely sexual in nature. Hugging friends and shaking hands with colleagues are other ways we communicate non-verbally in a non-sexual way. Caressing your loved one can be sensuous and sensual yet it need not be sexual. Explore touching each other in a playful way. Or why not sit quietly just being with each other?

One fun way to communicate is through toning, or sound, such as humming and overtones. The next time you have a conflict, try to tone your emotions, without using words. Begin by focusing inwards then breathe softly and let the sound come naturally on the out breath. If you let the sound come naturally you won't strain your vocal chords.

Instead of dialoguing at your next meeting, try painting and drawing your ideas. Focus on conveying the feeling in your drawing, then try to put it into words. Let yourself play with different ways to get your ideas across. Experiment with gestures and body language, or use music to enhance the communication process, or why not dance and movement?

Getting verbal

We've finally arrived at the mode of communication most practiced – using words to make ourselves understood. We talk on the telephone, we read and write with words be it letters or emails, sms or text messages, posts on Facebook, we listen to the words in movies and on television. Let's face it, words make up the better part of how we communicate.

So how do we best communicate with one another? How do we have a dialogue that is of mutual benefit? I think one key word is curiosity. To be curious about the other person, how they think, how they feel and what they value. Also to be curious about ourselves. If we can go into dialogues without a set goal or outcome to achieve other than to have a conversation to deepen the understanding between us, we could change so much in this world. But how often does it happen?

When talking, it's important to be clear about boundaries. My thoughts are not your thoughts and vice versa. Instead of trying to convince the other of your viewpoint, try to find out why they have this viewpoint. What underlying values drive their viewpoint? How did they come to think this way? Have they always had this stance?

In Sweden, where I currently live, there is a strong push for consensus. To think alike and to agree is important. Needless to say there are many of my friends who are afraid to discuss politics at work, for fear that no-one else shares their viewpoint. My answer is, "the only way you will find out is to talk about your views. You may be surprised how many actually think like you, but were also afraid to speak up." I've encountered this at many meetings. I've lived in the US for far too many years to be able to shut up or to not think my own thoughts. I speak my mind. So often, after the meeting, one or more of my Swedish colleagues come up to me to say, "I'm so glad you said thus and such, I'm so glad you spoke up, I totally agree with you." At the meeting they hadn't said a word, and if I hadn't been there I doubt anyone else would have said a word. Makes me wonder how many decisions get made that do not have the support of the members. Quite a few I suspect, which may be the cause of the many difficulties in implementing changes in Swedish organizations. The disagreement comes out in resistance and quiet sabotage of the new direction, because the support was never there in the first place.

Dealing with the caveman

While we are on the subject of communication, I'd like to interject a strategy some of us females have found extremely useful when dealing with the typical male response of going into a cave, symbolically speaking. Perhaps the men would describe it as they need time or space to be alone, to sort their thoughts and feelings.

When you have emotions and the man in your life has swum out to sea, or gone into his cave, or floated away on a cloud, you don't have to hold your emotions in and wait for him to come back out. From experience, you know it may be some time before he reappears. I think they wait until your pesky emotions have died down and they feel it's safe to come out. It makes us feel like only positive emotions are ok, that to cry or be upset is cause for the caveman to appear. The mate of one of my friends always asks if she is through pouting, as if pouting is not an acceptable way to feel, as if when she is pouting it means there is something wrong between them.

What we've discovered is that the man really seems to need to go away into a cave. I need to go into a cave at times too. I don't feel social, I don't always want to talk to other people, I just want to be left alone. However we tend to encounter the caveman approach to emotions more with males than with females.

But never fear, there is a way to deal with this. Your emotions are up, you've just started to explore the depth of your emotions, and he disappears. Don't run after him, that won't solve anything. Pull yourself together, center yourself, reflect, then and only then, write down what you are feeling. It may help to paint your emotions to get to the bottom of your turmoil. Focus on communicating how you feel.

Entire books have been written on this one subject alone, but let me convey a few key principles. Be careful of making assumptions about his motives or second-guessing what is going on with him. You haven't a clue, and you may as well admit it. Focus on what you wish to happen and be totally aware that he may or may not want to grant your wishes. He isn't playing to the same script you are and you may as well face it now. Be honest about what actually upset you. If a childhood wound has been triggered, tell him this situation reminds you of a familiar pattern. Telling him that he has awakened an old wound is fine, to take all the accumulated woundedness you're carrying and dumping it on your partner is not ok. Here again is why therapy is so important. When old wounds are triggered, go get therapy, work through the stuff so you can get rid of it. Then go have a dialogue. And lastly it's not always about ourselves, about us having to change. It takes two to tango and if you are the one always bending and adjusting to someone with a take it or leave it attitude, it may be time to look around for another playmate.

When you've written to your caveman as clear as you can be about your feelings and wishes without blaming, leave him be, let him read and digest it at his own pace. He will eventually reappear. The cynic in me says he'll reappear when he gets horny or he thinks the coast is clear, he is missing you and he thinks enough time has elapsed that you have forgotten the whole thing and you can just get on with having a good time. When he does come out it would be nice to have a real dialogue. I often find that it's like starting over again, then by the time I get warmed up, he's off and gone, again.

I would love to get a male viewpoint here, how does it look from your perspective?

Sure, I want your body

I admit it. It's my physical desires that come alive first. So sure, I want your body, but I want to know what is in your heart and mind as well. The physical attraction gets my attention. Sparks my interest. Then I want to know more. Who you really are, what you think and care about, what you dream about, what you want with your life. I want to know what makes you happy and what makes you sad. What your childhood was like and what matters to you. How you deal with difficulties and where your focus is at work and play. I want to know all of you, not just the outer facade.

It's very important that you want to know who I really am. That you are curious about me and my thoughts and emotions and needs. One of my favorite movie lines comes from *A Room with a View*. He says, "when I hold you in my arms, I want you to think your own thoughts and have your own feelings." Now that's music to my ears.

School of Life

I propose that we need a *School of Life* where we can learn the really useful stuff one needs to live. I mean, how often have you had real use of the facts you had to learn in school? Do you really need to know all the kings and presidents, all the rivers, all the military battles, or do long division? Well, yes some of it is useful, but how about teaching children (or adults for that matter) how to talk to each other, how to take care of their bodies, what foods are good for you, how to grow a garden, balance a check book, you name it, all the essentials for a happy life. We may be much better off learning about how to care for a house, how to balance priorities, learning and discussing ethics and morality, how to be a responsible member of a community or what that means.

In a school of life we could have a very different curriculum. Imagine what the world would be like if we had a different approach to what is important to know and learn. What if we learned early on how to therapeutically work through our issues? If we grew up with an ingrained sense of our own rhythms and needs. How about if we didn't train children out of listening to their bodies, but instead showed them how to enhance their inner communication. What a different world it would be.

Wouldn't it be wonderful if we learned how to care for each other and ourselves - emotionally, physically, mentally and spiritually in an empowered way.

Fifteen

If I say what I need he'll leave

My friends are accustomed to me being available on short notice, to go off on trips or to come hang out at my house for a few weeks. The writing of this book is at a critical stage, the words and structure are really coming together and I feel a strong need to focus on writing. This is not a good time for me to take a week or more off. So I've had to say, "no" to several of my friends. I've had to say, "it's not convenient for me right now. In a few months, when the manuscript has gone to the publisher, then I will be free to roam around again." I've felt a fear as I've said this. A fear that my friend(s) will take off in a huff and not want to be my friend(s) anymore. My logical mind knows this is bullshit, but the feeling lingers and I probe my memory banks of what situation this reminds me of. My dreams help me along and up comes a memory from the distant past.

When I was at University I dated a guy for about a year and a half. Let's call him Jerry, to give him a name. Before I met him, I had been quite sexually active, as most of us were in the early seventies. I was on birth control pills for that very reason. Jerry was very good looking. I remember my roommate came looking for me to tell me Jerry was trying to find me so he could ask me out. Her demeanor was very much, "this is important, one of the best catches in my class wants to ask you out." When Jerry caught up with me, he asked me out, to a Who concert.

We started dating. He was very generous, taking me out to dinner, movies, we went skiing, to concerts and to church. Jerry was quite religious and close to his mother and family, he talked to Jesus on a regular basis. Part of the package was that he wanted to be a virgin on his wedding night. Ah yes, you might say, I see problems ahead for Eva. Well, I'm open to other ideas and willing to experiment. Not until today, more than thirty years later, do I understand the full impact of our relationship and how it ended.

As we got closer, we started necking and petting but it was never a question of going further. He would get a release, but he didn't seem to understand that I also had needs. He would talk about how wonderful it was to ejaculate. But it was always on his terms. There wasn't a question of me having needs. I tried time and time again to say that as a woman, I also needed orgasms and to be touched. He would kiss me and hold me as he rubbed against me but that was about it. Today I would be direct - I want this and this and I want it in this way. But I was young. I became more and more frustrated, as I wasn't getting my needs met.

I explored his ideas about sex and what they were about and why he wanted to wait. Well it made sense that he wanted to respect the wedding vows that were so sacred to him. Then I wondered, what if we weren't sexually compatible? What a horrible thought to discover that on your wedding night.

Finally one night, I think it might even have been New Year's Eve, I brought the subject up, "we have to talk about this." I remember being nervous and eating a whole bag of chocolate covered raisins. I launched into the conversation with, "I need to understand your thinking about sex and I don't want to wait until our wedding night." He explained to me that sex was something special, not just some animal thing you do. In his head, sex in marriage was "Honey, let's make a baby tonight." The realization of what he was saying sunk in, he didn't just want to wait until marriage, but then sex would only be for procreation! He wasn't even catholic! Oh dear I thought, we really need to sort this out.

"Do you really think that is reasonable?" I said, "to only have sex when we want to make babies? What about all the other times we feel tender and heaven forbid just plain horny and full of lust?" Poor Jerry was so indoctrinated by his church teachings that he couldn't conceive of having sex with me unless we were married and about to make a baby.

It dawned on me that I was waiting for very meager satisfaction of my rather healthy lusts. As we talked, Jerry got more and more upset. I was challenging everything he stood for and believed in. His conclusion was angrily, "you want me to screw you" and then he broke up with me. Left me high and dry. Stunned into silence, I vowed something that isn't quite released yet. But he taught me unequivocally that if I make my needs known, he would leave. I was not allowed to have any needs, no sir. No wonder that set me up for later disasters.

I was really hurt but didn't process it at the time. I think I was too stunned to be able to. That's what happens when you are in shock. You go numb and can't deal with the emotions and you end up carrying them with you.

These beliefs I've carried with me into other relationships. Beliefs like "if I tell him how I feel I'm afraid he'll leave and not come back" or "if I show my needs, he will think I'm being difficult and break off the communication."

I have a friend who says my needs are so overwhelming that no one can meet them. I think she is talking about herself and her own experience that she can't get her needs met and if she shows the slightest neediness people leave. Yes my needs are surfacing, and for some people that is scary but it's also a cleansing process of relationships. I am practicing stating what I need but it doesn't mean that others have to fulfill them.

Unconsciously, I have chosen partners where I can't get too close and who aren't into meeting my needs. Oh, wouldn't it be wonderful if everyone could get therapy on a regular basis and we could work through issues like these as we go along instead of filing them in bags and carrying them with us for years and years and years.

I would love to see therapy taught from a perspective of giving you the tools to use for your own healing and to practice with the other members of the class. As issues come up we could help each other. We would take turns and would come together as equals. Many people trained and certified in alternative therapies have done the training for their own inner process, not to make a living at. Why not teach it from that perspective to begin with?

Jerry blamed me for our break-up. He laid the guilt on me and left me a message that my sexual needs were way out of line. Boo-hoo, it used to be my favorite pastime. I am experiencing an intense anger towards Jerry and very deep hurt. Guilt and shame as well. Like my sexual needs were not ok, something dirty we shouldn't talk about.

He projected his shit onto me. Why couldn't he have said we have different opinions about this? Why couldn't we have recognized that we have different values and we need to part amicably and work through this? That's the trouble with break-ups, they often leave all kinds of unfinished baggage and it only pops back up again when it's triggered like now, some thirty years later. Sigh.

Exploring the other viewpoint

When we have a conflict, if we could only stop to explore the other viewpoint, we would at least be able to have a dialogue about it. But, as in the example above, one or the other goes off in a huff, because all of a sudden something has popped up that wasn't in the script in their head of how things should be. Why do we humans find it so difficult to communicate basic ideas and thoughts?

We are so advanced technologically. We have made great strides in developing our physical bodies, just look at the athletes today. We have come a long way in our understanding of many things, except human relationships. It's like we expect that to take care of itself. The most important issue, the glue that holds it all together, is our relationships with each other, yet most of us spend minimal time making the relationships we do have work.

It is true that none of us have received the appropriate training. Perhaps it's because we don't really know how? We can start, right where we are at. The next time someone offers an opinion different from yours, go at it from a detective stance. Ask questions seeking to understand their viewpoint. Have a dialogue about the different viewpoints around the table, seek to understand how each of you arrived at where you are now.

Then ask yourselves, which part of you holds these beliefs? Is it your head? Is it your heart? Is it your body? Is it your Soul? These questions alone should stimulate an interesting dialogue.

A letter not sent

When we can't have a dialogue, when it is not possible to sort it out with the other person, we can write a letter. Depending on what and how you write it, you may or may not want to send it. The letter writing process is primarily for your own sorting, so you can heal the hurt and move on. Most letters we write in this fashion should not be sent. I've written tons that have gone into the trash, where they belong. Heaping our anger on another serves no real purpose, does it? You know all too well how it feels when someone heaps his or her trash on you. It feels like yuck. The deep mucky stuff belongs in the therapy process. It's one thing to point out that your wounds have been triggered, it's another entirely to take all of your past wounds and hurts and heaping your pain on your partner.

However, there are times when the most appropriate response is to let it rip, to really let the other person have it. Tune in to your inner guidance on this. In abuse cases some say confront, others say not to confront. I don't think there can be a set rule about this. In some cases it's appropriate, in others not. Check in and feel what is right for you in each situation. Ultimately you are the one responsible for all your actions.

In the example with Jerry above, we never had the chance to have a dialogue. Our viewpoints were so diverse that we couldn't even discuss them. I'm astounded to realize the depth of the pain that remains in me. No wonder I'm terrified to reveal my inner self. No wonder I worry about rejection. No wonder I'm at a loss for words.

Well better late than never. After more than thirty years I feel it's time to remedy the situation by writing a letter. I'm including it here, to illustrate how one can write to squeeze out the hurt and confusion so at least you can heal. It does not feel appropriate to mail this letter. It's my process. Use your own judgment when and what to send, if at all.

Dear Jerry,

I know it's more than thirty years since we broke up. But as the saying goes, better late than never. I had no idea I still carried so much pain and confusion from our breakup. I have not placed much significance on our relationship at all in all my therapy work, and when you've come up, I've worked through the issue and thought I was done. But in hindsight I realize the issues have been deep and to be honest you've come up several times. For some reason most of the stuff I've had to work through on my own, going deep into my emotions and beliefs, working with dreams and various pains in my body.

It's time to say all the things I didn't say, that I should have said way back when. I was so naive then, had no idea how to make sure my needs got met. On the surface you were such a perfect catch. You were a gentleman, very good looking, you took me out to dinners and football games, to concerts and church outings and included me in your family get togethers. What was there to complain about?

Good question. Partly it's about my needs, partly it's about underlying values, and most of all it's about beliefs of what life is all about. I don't know how to start this, where to begin, how to nail down the real issue. I'll start at the end, when I brought up my sexual needs, and you simply walked off. That hurt, excruciatingly. I felt rejected at the core of my being. I felt I had no right to have needs. I felt my wishes weren't important. I felt like a monster. I felt betrayed. I felt sad and angry and I felt guilty. I felt that my sexual needs were perverse, that there was something inherently bad with my bodily lusts, that I wouldn't fit in somehow. I felt I wasn't marriage material. I felt abandoned.

I have experienced great difficulty in sharing my inner self with another, for fear they will do what you did – simply get up and leave. I have been so afraid of being left, that I have put up with some really awful behavior. I never wanted to be alone, but that is what I am. I haven't known how deep my pain has been. I haven't understood how deeply you hurt me. To simply leave, no discussion, no dialogue, to just get up and walk out when I show you my desires, that really hurt. I am most afraid of revealing the inner sanctity, the inner space that is tender and vulnerable for fear that the next man will do the same, just get up and leave.

I know I will get hurt again, that is part of the earth plane. But I would like to be able to have a dialogue, to be able to explore our viewpoints, to understand each other. Because at the bottom of it all, that is what we didn't do. We never spent time trying to understand where the other one was coming from, or discussing what we wanted out of life, if we were to spend it together. It feels as if when I did surface the discussion, I was rejected outright. In a way your message to me was if I had known this from the start I never would have spent time with you. I felt worthless and rejected.

And you know what? I would find it hard to believe that you and your wife have only made love when you made babies. I would hazard to guess you have discovered your ideals were not upholdable after all. That reality put sex in a much different light for you. But I guess I will never know. And I suppose it's not important for me to find out, I just tend to be curious about everything.

I have experienced guilt and a feeling of not being able to breathe, I gasp for air as I try to comprehend what you were saying. I felt like your views would suffocate me. And of course they would have if we'd stayed together. I hope to God I have finally cleared out the cobwebs and totally cleaned house as far as our relationship is concerned. I want to forgive you for the pain you have caused me and I hope you have forgiven me as well. Because I do understand it couldn't have been easy for you either, to be faced with me who so not fit into your ideal of how a woman should be. Must have been quite a shock to you.

All my best/Eva

PS – I might as well stamp reject on my forehead. That is how I feel. Like a reject. It certainly has played out that way in my life. And I've set myself up to be rejected time and time again. At least I have found the cause and can heal it, but it sure hurts. I find myself astounded at the depth of the pain and how this has been lurking there for so many years. I have dug and dug in therapy. Perhaps I am scraping bottom – at long last!

PS #2 – You know, it's your loss. I am a wonderful woman. I am a treasure for someone who knows how to appreciate me. Life goes on and we all get our just deserts.

As you can see there were emotional remnants that surfaced in the writing. One never knows what will come up or out. The best advice I can give is to just write, don't censor, and simply let the words flow. If the tears overwhelm you, pause, and let them flow. If anger surfaces, go find a pillow to beat on and sit with the feeling deep in your body until it has passed through. Make sure you squeeze out all the bits and pieces so you can be done with them. Keep in mind that it can take a few turns, deep hurts often take many layers to work through. Instead of reacting with, "no, not that issue again," see it as another step on your healing journey. Each time you work on an issue, you will see that it alters, there is another aspect you are working on. Sometimes the differences are subtle, sometimes big. The only way out of it is by going through it, that I can say for sure.

What do I know?

Who am I to pretend I know enough about the subject of relationships to write a whole book? Well, I can't say I've had a life long marriage that works, quite the contrary. I've had lots of friends and lovers and have pondered the meaning of it all. Perhaps we look at it from the wrong perspective. Maybe, the goal is not to find your partner and glom onto him, or, as we say in business, find your niche and stay there. Perhaps the whole game is about finding new ways to look at relationships. If an experience lasts a lifetime or a fleeting moment, what difference does it make? Is the value we place on an experience measured by the time we spent in it? Food for thought.

I think there is no right or wrong way. Each one of us has to find out what is important for us and live our lives accordingly. For some, life long marriages are the path to salvation and deep growth, for others, it is something else entirely. There is nothing inherently better or worse with one alternative or another, the most important is to be true to ourselves.

I have been made to feel very wrong about my choices, criticized by others and myself for failing at relationships. Before I could start this book

I had to emotionally release that feeling of failure. As the tears washed down my face, facing my feeling of failure, something deep inside me released. Perhaps I had been looking at it from the wrong angle? I had tried to make myself fit into a norm and pattern imposed by society. But did this fit me? Why would it, when everything else in my life was about breaking patterns? I became an engineer when only 2% of my class were women. I was the first woman engineer at Scott Paper in Everett, WA and became their first woman engineering supervisor. At one of our international meetings my Spanish counterpart walked up to me and asked, "whose wife are you?" I didn't fit any molds then, and I certainly don't now. After all, my spiritual name is Pathfinder.

So it's not so strange that I should write a book about breaking relationship molds. Many years ago I attended a talk by Jennifer James, a well-known anthropologist from Seattle. She said women can now get their own antelope at the grocery store, but we still act as if we are dependent on the man to bring it home. How true. Our assumptions and expectations about relationships have not kept pace with the changes in our lives.

In my second book I wrote about some of my relationships and my longing to connect at a deeper level. To connect emotionally, mentally, physically and spiritually. Interestingly enough, many people assumed I meant I was looking for a marriage, live together and stay together situation. That isn't what I said. I said I want to connect. I didn't specify for how long or how frequent. I want to be free to be myself and I want to connect with the other person's true self. I want to let go of all the roles we play. There is work to do here. In every meeting there is a mirror of the unhealed parts of ourselves, opportunities to grow and discover.

Do I have a clue how to do this? Of course not. But I want to explore the assumptions and learn how to have relationships based on truth.

Assumed rights

I was seeing this man, let's call him Billy. We'd been together since September, he didn't live with me but spent much of his free time at my house. As Valentine's Day approached my friends would ask me what plans we had. I'd answer, "I don't know, Billy hasn't said anything." I kept waiting for him to make plans or ask, "what would you like to do for Valentines?" but nothing was mentioned. Valentines Day fell on a Saturday that year. I puttered around the house, and at 4 or 5 in the afternoon Billy calls. By this time I had assumed we weren't getting together as no plans had been made. He wanted to come over. I remember I wasn't in a very receptive mood, said something like, "what for?" He chose not to hear that and came over anyway. Right there, I should have had a dialogue about my expectations and that I was not pleased and quite frankly wasn't in the mood to have him come over. I had really wanted to go out or have something romantic planned. But I wasn't very feisty then. At least not in my private life.

So Billy comes over, he's bought flowers. At this point I don't remember if I fixed dinner or if he came over afterwards. I do remember we ended up making love on the floor, but I really didn't want to. I kept scooting away from him. I was pissed at him. I felt taken for granted, that he could just assume I would be home and ready and willing - I didn't take him out of that misconception did I? Like I say, I was not good at verbalizing what was going on inside me then.

OK, it obviously wasn't just Billy's fault that this happened. I wasn't clear about my expectations or how I felt. I swallowed my emotions. Now Billy could have been more suave and taken me out or at the very least said, "Honey, Valentine's is coming up, what would you like to do?" I may have liked to stay home and do a special meal or gone out, the activity is not the most important here. It's being left hanging, not knowing if we were even getting together. And the *assumed right* of just showing up whenever.

Just one more example where having a dialogue, really seeking to understand each other could have made this Valentine's very special for both of us. In hindsight, we would have done our relationship much good if we had spent the evening talking to each other instead of glossing it over by having sex.

You know, writing this is not easy. I feel like a twit, it makes me look stupid, but oh well. One of the reasons I leave in so many embarrassing details about myself is I have discovered there are so many of my friends who have had similar experiences. Which leads me to believe that many of my readers have also done stupid things. My hope is that by writing about mine will help you heal and release your past. Together we can toss the sack of shame out the window.

Sixteen

Fascinated with groups

You may have guessed by now that I am fascinated by groups and their organization. I've participated in a number of groups where there hasn't been a traditional leader. Each group has been unique in its make-up, purpose and focus.

When a friend of mine bemoaned the difficulty in running her own business, I helped her start a group named the Cottage Industries Board of Directors. She was the only one employed in her company and she had several friends in the same boat. The purpose of the group was to help support each other and function much like a Board of Directors would in a large company. Here they could test ideas and learn from each other.

I've participated in several groups where the leaders started out teaching the material for their own enjoyment. In time the leaders started their own businesses offering workshops and individual coaching. The time spent just playing and sharing helped form the foundation for their business successes.

One of the organizations I belonged to would meet once a month for a program and potluck. Not only did we get to learn new tools, we made new friends as well. Never underestimate the social needs of groups. We need social time to build relationships before we get to work the deeper issues.

My friends with the gemstone passion held Open Houses every month. It became a Sunday afternoon gathering place for many of us and we did learn much about gemstones and became good customers. If what you are selling is new and different and takes more than a thirty-second sound bite to sell (that covers most of us) an Open House is a good way to go. Out of this group the *Life Mission* and *Spa Healing Temple* projects were formed. One thing leads to another, but you have to start somewhere.

My involvement with various committees at the Swedish Cultural Center all came out of meeting another member the same age as me and with the same passion for putting life into organizations. We started talking and generating ideas and set up a meeting with the Board to present our thoughts. Before we knew it we were involved in planning events, redesigning the nominations process and getting more volunteers involved than ever before. The power of one plus one, is not two, as in simple arithmetic, it is more like ten.

Another group grew out of a shared interest in creative dance. There had been a leader and teacher, but she moved away to another city. We decided to continue the group, without a leader. Doing a leaderless group works well if the group is small, you all know each other and have gone through "basic training" so to speak. In the beginning we would decide on a theme for the next gathering. Each one would bring music, exercises and ideas on that theme. We would start with a sharing, then talk about how we wanted the music and theme to flow, and get going. In time the group became so in tune that we simply let intuition guide us from week to week. The work was spread out among us, one would bring the stereo, another kept track of the key and rent money and so on. There was also the opportunity for us to lead a whole session and experiment, when the spirit moved us to do so. We met for two hours every week.

The last few years I've been a part of a painting group. Everyone in the group has taken the basic instruction in Vedic Art, a process where you paint intuitively from within. We meet one weekend a month to paint and socialize. Sometimes we play music to enhance our process, or use silence, meditation or intention to lead our work. Other times we simply paint for the joy of painting. We have jointly purchased paints and other supplies. Continuing to work in a group after you have taken a basic course is a very good way to deepen your knowledge of the process. It's something I highly recommend.

If I were to do any teaching again, it's this very concept I would like to seed. Teach you the basics and then have you continue working with each other. It would be a great way to do therapy training, because you would learn tools for life, which you could use with each other. A vision for the future?

Play with Possibilities

For some time I had wished for a group where we could combine dancing, painting, toning, philosophizing and meditating in a free and flowing manner. I had tried to enthuse my painting group, but they really wanted to focus on painting. Then I went to a get together of the Vedic artists in another town. As part of the program we danced. Yes, how exciting. So in the course of things I mentioned my dream of a combination group. I felt that so many of us had explored separate processes and now it was time to weave them together. One of the people there became so enthralled with the idea she went out and found a space for us to meet in, which would be ideal for this kind of group. She didn't feel like organizing the actual pulling together for the group, but I did.

An invitation to explore was included in my next email newsletter. I knew from experience to nail down some parameters for people to get hold of:

Group for dancing-painting-singing etc?

For a long time I have dreamt of having a self steering group where we get together to dance, paint, tone, meditate, philosophize etc. Now it appears the time has come to join with kindred spirits in this adventure. We have found a space to use, rent free, which is quite suitable for these kinds of activities.

This is not a group for beginners. It is for those of you who have experience in one or more of the following areas: intuitive painting, creative dance, toning, meditation and/or personal growth and have the will to deepen your own development. My idea is that we meet one weekend a month between 10am and 4pm and that we rotate the leadership. If you feel shy about taking on a leadership role at the start, there is always something you can help with, such as being the keeper of keys, keeping track of the participant list or being a "cheerleader" giving moral support. More than one person can take on the leadership for a weekend, it's an excellent way to test your capabilities to team up with one or more persons.

In a group like this, there will be triggers of your own inner processes. It is assumed that you have some experience and comfort level with working on yourself.

I propose we meet these four weekends...

I will happily take the leadership role the first weekend.

Does this sound interesting? Forward this to your friends and colleagues.

Let me know if you want to lead a weekend. Sign up now for this exciting group!

The response was overwhelming. The time was really ripe for this. And as I had wished, the geographic spread of participants was like a star from the center and the mix of capabilities and experience was rich. How lovely. Right away there was a volunteer to lead weekend number two, on the theme "creative dance and process painting."

In kicking around ideas about the group, I kept talking about playing with possibilities and all of a sudden I realized, there was the name for our group *Play with Possibilities*. What a freeing concept.

As the first weekend drew near I pondered how I would lead it. While walking in the woods I was inspired with a focal thread – we needed to tune in the first weekend. What better way than to play with toning exercises like HU sing and toning each other's names. I got a rough structure for the weekend, but in order to do this work you have to stay in the moment and go with what is there and wants to happen. I had done this often enough in evening talks and shorter courses, but I hadn't yet done a whole weekend in free flow.

By the time the weekend rolled around, we were seventeen registered participants, twelve showed up. Two people arrived a half hour late – who were typically very punctual. Hmm, exploring opposites...

I was tested as well. There was one participant in particular who wanted to take over and dabble in my paint pot. I had to firmly set limits, "when you lead a weekend, you can do whatever you want to, but this time I am the leader. I make the decisions this weekend."

I had purposely stayed away from putting a candle in the center of our sharing circle, nor did I want some guru symbol there either. I wanted this start to truly reflect the purpose of playing with possibilities. For the same reason I used a stuffed animal, a Dalmatian puppy named Lucas, as our talking stick. I let him represent the focus on curiosity with no agenda or expectations.

We used the talking dog exercise to do a sharing. Now I'm sure you've all been to courses where the sharing goes on and on, and it gets really heavy. I wanted to stay away from the usual present ourselves and our qualifications. We weren't here to show how organized and capable we were. Just about all the participants were leaders and therapists, they already knew how to take charge and be serious, in spades.

I like to nip things in the bud, so I asked them to share the answer to three questions, "What is your name? Where do you come from? Why do you think you are here?" Short and sweet.

After our brief sharing, I read a passage from Carolina Eastwood's website with her interpretation of the full moon that weekend:

Full moon brings new realizations and changes
A full moon coupled with Jupiter in Virgo occurs on March 6. Opposing the moon-Jupiter coupling is the sun and Mercury in Pisces standing in a tense aspect with transformative Pluto in Sagittarius, an astrological milieu designed to bring significant realization and changes for those who are willing to do the necessary inner work. Using our brilliant mental capacity to discern solutions, plan strategically, and implement flawlessly can bring impressive results, but the question is posed at this full moon: To what purpose? The inner motivation behind every choice and action will determine our results. The degree of true happiness and fulfillment we experience in life comes in direct proportion to the quality of wisdom and love we act from. This full moon cautions us to be very clear in our intentions before acting.

Taking this moon message into our hearts, we did a HU sing followed by a brief meditation. We then spent the time until lunch painting in silence with a focus on that intention.

My original game plan had been to sing and tone our names after lunch, but as I felt into it, there seemed to be something else that needed to happen. There had been the two punctual types who had arrived a half-hour late in the morning. A couple who is habitually late came back early from lunch. Another aspect of exploring the other side, the opposite. Then another participant walks in, stops at my painting and exclaims, "oh what I could bring out in that painting! My fingers itch to go into it and lift out the details. I would never do that of course, dabble in someone else's painting!" At that moment, inspiration hit me. We would spend the afternoon exploring the very thing we normally don't do. I normally would not allow anyone to dabble in my painting and she wouldn't let herself do it. So I started by saying, "go ahead." At first she felt scared, "oh no I couldn't" then I coaxed the playful, explorer artist, and she plunged ahead. The rest of the group sat in stunned silence, there were some objections, some questions and after some hesitation the energy took off.

I normally wouldn't do leaderless for fear of chaos that might ensue. Each person was free to do what he or she wanted.

"Gee, what would I want to do?" they asked themselves. One asked, "is it restricted to painting or can I put on music and dance?" You can do anything you want on the theme of "not my normal behavior."

One put on music, I just floated around, joined the dancers. Another led a structured song, a sort of game I usually find challenging. I joined in. Then I felt a twinge as the "leader" to go check in how everyone was doing, and let go of that thought. I realized, "no I don't need to take care of them." Some sat quietly. One complained that she felt like she had already done this type of exercise and wasn't happy.

I had to let go of my fear that total chaos would break out - ah yes a bit of control to let go of...

Afterwards we did a short sharing to close out the day. One had felt totally paralyzed at first, "what do I want to do that I normally wouldn't do?" Another was unhappy, she just sat there when she really wanted to dance, and painted in her little space. Yet another loves circles and round forms, she decided to draw lines and geometric shapes. She showed us a beautiful drawing in soft pastels, all straight lines. She had discovered that straight lines could be beautiful and soft. But she still liked circles best. Someone else felt so free to just sit there with no expectation, no production, just puttering at their table like at preschool. Another would have sat quietly at her table when little, now she joined in the dancing and games. All in all it was a wonderful afternoon.

My fellow artist had pulled out details in my painting I never would have been able to. We signed the joint effort. I have this idea we should get together and paint for peace. Can you imagine Bush and Blair and Usama and Saddam each adding his energy to a joint painting for peace? The founder of Vedic Art, Curt Källman, has this vision of two armies poised for battle on the field. In we rush with our easels in between them and paint in that space between the warring sides. Lovely thoughts.

On Sunday I did a brief check in using talking dog. After a few shares the space went quiet and it felt like it was time for the next something. The person who had complained about the exercises on Saturday and had wanted things her way didn't show on Sunday, she had the stomach flu. Emotional issues were churning in her stomach.

I explained name singing and how to weave in intention. I wished to continue the theme of transformative full moon and to get to know one another. The name singing was powerful and varied.

After lunch we ended up sitting around and just chatting until it was time to go. The conversation was relaxed, easy, explorative and it flowed naturally. We had our chairs pulled around in a scattered fashion, yet we were all in a circle. It felt very comfortable.

We had succeeded in laying the foundation for a group that could really explore and play with possibilities. The concept was off to a great start to be tested and perhaps brought out into the world. I felt like the igniters, or the starters had come together and the work we were doing would be taken back to their places and reverberate out into the world.

It's Monday as I write this, the day after. This morning I woke up and danced, shook out a lot out of my arms and hands. I knew I needed to capture the essence of what we had done this weekend.

I feel a quiet satisfaction, content. You know how after some courses you feel euphoric, or processed? This was the in between, just being in contentment and ease. This is how life was meant to be.

It's important that we carefully laid the groundwork and built the trust. Letting ourselves open at a mellow pace. Next month is digging deep and that feels so appropriate.

Paint without Purpose

After playing with possibilities I sorted and pondered and laid on the couch staring into space, did some spring-cleaning, which is an important part of any process. Before the new can come in, we have to clean out the old. And sure enough, a new creative idea popped in, inspired by a series of events.

When I moved back to Sweden in the late 90's I had no idea I would end up teaching toning. I had participated in weekly toning groups for about four years in Seattle with Marline Lesh and Diana Nielsen and went to the monthly gatherings of the Sound Healers of Washington. I did it because it was fun. I enjoyed it. I liked the groups and it helped me open up my throat and find my voice. When I started I firmly believed what I had been told all my life, "you can't carry a tune." When my friend told me about the toning group I shyly asked if I could come too. Everyone else was trained in voice or music or communication and I had no training and I thought I had no talent. They said, "yes, of course you are welcome."

So I went and discovered that I do indeed have a voice and I can tone quite well. Hmmm... so it is when you do something just for yourself without attachment to the outcome.

Funny how the universe prepares you. I teach from a presence, in the now, perspective, that this is something we all can do. All we need to do is get out of the way, relax, and let our bodies remember how to do it. No forcing, keep breathing in and out until the sound comes naturally. One woman sat through a whole semester without making a sound.

Another thread was my mail to my friend, meet without expectation, to explore our connection without any preconceived ideas of where we were going or why.

Then the weekend of play, letting it unfold in the present. And the strong message or idea that I wanted to do courses again. The trick was finding the thread, or focus, that excited my life energy. What I have learned about getting groups together is that it can't be completely leaderless and it needs a focus, thread or main theme.

Since the year 2000 I have been painting with a Vedic Art group. We meet one weekend a month and I do it for fun, to have some social contact, get to play with colors and just be. In Vedic Art there are seventeen principles that lead you to the state of *I am*. To be honest, I never have been able to sort the principles and translate them into what I do, I just paint from the inside out. I paint my feelings, my thoughts, my consciousness or whatever is there in the now. If someone is talking to me while I paint, our dialogue goes into the painting.

When I had explained to the Play with Possibilities group the intention to paint our wish under silence, the Vedic Art teacher in our group clarified that the intention I had so eloquently described was principle #6, if I remember correctly. I thought, "oh is that what it is? Here I have been painting this process for four years and I still don't have the principles straight." Does it matter? No, when you paint intuitively, you don't need the one, two, three, etc. The steps are there to help you achieve the *I am* state.

I'm reminded of a chiropractor I used to see. He did beautiful drawings and etchings. He had started with an instruction book with step-by-step exercises. First he was to draw an egg shape. No matter how hard he tried, he couldn't for the life of him draw an egg. Before he pitched the book in the trashcan, he flipped through the rest of the book. On the last page was an exercise to draw an old man, with beard and wrinkles. He thought, "I could do that!" And proceeded to draw the old man, just like in the book. He was a natural artist. Which brings up the question, how do you teach creativity?

I believe you teach it by doing. What has been helpful both with toning and painting is doing it in group with other people of varying skill levels. We learn from each other, techniques and approaches, and we support each other in the growth process.

Then I thought, I wonder if my painting is like my toning. I've been doing it for fun, but maybe it is what I am to teach. Because I would teach painting like toning. Your body knows how to do this. I'll help you let go and set the stage so you can be free and creative. Out of all this a new course idea was born.

New Course - Paint without Purpose

with Eva Dillner

We'll explore intuitive painting where there is no goal, no agenda, no expectation of a finished product. There are no techniques to learn, no right or wrong way to do this. Bring your curiosity and your art supplies.

It doesn't matter if you use crayons, pastels, acrylics or watercolors nor what size your canvas is. This course is about playful exploration of who you are inside. No previous experience necessary.

To facilitate the process we may meditate, tone, dance and philosophize as befits the group

By letting go of the attachment to an outcome, by being present and willing to explore, we can unearth hidden aspects of ourselves. When we relax and let go anything can happen.

How many times have you chewed and stewed over a problem only to have the solution drop in when you least expected it?

The writing of this book has taken priority and I'm not sure this course will ever happen, but if you don't try out new ideas nothing will ever get off the ground.

Seventeen

PAGIC, like magic

Bet you've never heard of *pagic*. I hadn't either until a friend of mine helped me form the acronym. Pagic is pronounced like magic. It stands for

Planning

Analysis

Growth

Interaction

Creativity

These are the ingredients I need in a job to be satisfied. I had worked at the Everett plant for over ten years. I had worked my way through the interesting jobs in engineering and logistics/procurement and realized that what I really wanted, was to work internationally. One friend said, "that's the most sensible idea you have come up with so far." To him, that made more sense than anything else I had been considering. I had also had an affair with this guy, so you could say he knew me pretty well.

I went to see my friend in personnel. He laughed and told me, "sure, when I'm Manager of International HR! Eva, you can't get there from here. You have to go to corporate headquarters first and network there, then you can go overseas."

Not to be daunted, I had to go ponder what I might want to do at corporate headquarters before I could make my dreams come true. I decided I wanted to check out marketing. I set up some exploratory meetings through a mentor in procurement. As part of my preparation for this trip I developed *pagic*.

What is fascinating with these kinds of exercises is how well they fit over time. Pagic is as valid today as it was then. It carries across all the functional designations. I think it is a more valuable tool for matching employees to jobs than our traditional descriptions.

To do the exercise for yourself, look at the ingredients that satisfy and excite you in a job. Once you have a list of words, narrow them down to a manageable number. See if you can make an acronym out of the first letter of each quality. Having an acronym simplifies remembering the list. In an interview, under pressure, it's to your advantage to be able to succinctly summarize what qualities you bring to the position.

Up the down staircase

Getting from here to there is not always a logical progression. I went to corporate headquarters to see about a job in marketing so I could network my way overseas. I didn't get a job in marketing. I was offered a job in France. One that didn't exist before. Because I had been showing an interest in moving on I was present in the decision makers minds when they searched around for suitable candidates.

I ended up where I was supposed to go albeit in a roundabout way. So many of the other people on this project had similar experiences. It felt as if we were a group of souls called together for this gathering.

One colleague worked at corporate headquarters. As he was going down the escalator at lunch time, he saw another manager coming up the escalator, who called out, "What are you working with these days?" "Not much," was his reply. Next, he was asked, "how would you like to go to London?" to which he replied, "well maybe." The other manager said, "why don't you come up to my office and we'll talk about it?" So he did. Three days later he was on his way to London. He had happened to pass by when the manager was stewing on his problem of finding a suitable candidate to send. I don't think it is coincidence. I think it is our Higher Selves directing us where we need to go.

Another guy was walking down the hallway when a group of managers were discussing where on earth they could find a French-speaking employee who understood manufacturing and paper machine construction. In unison, they yelled out "there he is!" The answer literally walked by their door. Talk about having the solution handed to you on your doorstep.

Empowerment

You know how irritating it is to get advice you haven't asked for. The underlying assumption is that the other person knows better than you. Or take the software, Microsoft Word. It automatically changes things you haven't asked it to do. Nowhere in the basic instruction manual do they tell you how to set up the basic formatting the way you want it and how to keep those settings. It is the number one complaint in my circle of friends, "how do you turn the bloody thing off?" The programmers at Microsoft are trying to do the thinking for us. It makes me feel disempowered, because the program goes in and dabbles in my paint pot without my permission.

Empowerment is key when working with me. Without empowerment you will remain stuck in the old world. In the new world, we are truly equals. What do I mean by equals? One example I like to use is teaching. If you you teach as a facilitator, you are part of the process. You too are allowed to fall apart, to be natural. When you teach as a facilitator, you don't have to shut off the natural flow of energy. On the other hand, in traditional teaching you are meant to be an authority, to have control of your class, to present material as if it is the truth with a capital T. You are not encouraged to show your emotions or share your own process. Mostly it's about showing how competent and clever you are. Ok, I know it, I'm on my soapbox. But the subject of authority versus empowerment is a very key concept in my view of the world.

From Social Democrats to Kalki

In the Swedish language, the word empowerment does not exist. The societal structure is based on social democracy, where the government is assumed to know best, and it's practically impossible to make your own decisions when dealing with the state provided services. One friend describes it as either something is mandatory or it's forbidden. Swedes love authority and to be told what to do. It's like the government is one big parent and the population is made up of little children, who can't think for themselves.

So it's not surprising that the latest Indian guru, Kalki, has gathered such an enormous following here. The Swede is so used to getting the answer from an authority, that the very notion that the answer lies within, that you can have your own connection to God, does not compute. So instead of living your life according to the dictates of a political party, you switch allegiance and follow a guru. I have no opinion on the spiritual teachings of Kalki. I believe in listening to and reading from many sources, then retaining what rings true in my heart.

I don't believe we need an interpreter, or intermediary, to tell us what to do. I like to do my own thinking. It's one thing to listen to different philosophers, it's another to give away your power to them. And it's so easy to do. You take a class, listen to a speaker, and get enthused. It's so easy to swallow it all hook, line and sinker, without screening the whole rote of the message. If you find yourself quoting some master or teacher, stop and ask yourself, "do I know this to be true from my own experience, or am I simply parroting what I've been taught?" It's so easy to become a parrot, I know, I've been there lots of times. Which is why I'm making such a point of it here. You need to find your own truth and stand on your own two feet in order to fulfill your mission on earth. As long as you're parroting someone else's truth, you aren't really free.

I've known many people who belong to "guru" type organizations, like Osho, Eckankar and SRF (which I lightheartedly refer to as the Yogananda Club). My friends have willingly shared their beliefs and described what their organizations are all about, but I've never felt pressured to join. I've not felt like they were trying to sell me anything. We were simply exchanging different views and possibilities. There is a different dynamic with the disciples of Kalki that I've met. It may simply be over enthusiasm on their part in the newness. However, the unstatistical sampling I'm referring to have been intent on selling me on their religion. Wanting to give me deeksha (aka diksha), wanting me to come to the satsangs and so on. Repeatedly asking me even after I've clearly stated I'm not interested.

One of my pet peeves is someone trying to convince me after I've said no. I respect your opinion and your right to be different from me, so please respect my no when I say it. I shouldn't have to repeat it over and over. Do you think you can wear me down, like water on a rock? That if you pester me long enough I will come around? Perhaps pausing and examining your deeper motivations would do you a world of good?

Unequal relationships

The traditional way of looking at relationships like:

> client – therapist
>
> disciple – guru
>
> pupil – teacher

child – parent

lover – healer

implies that one is in authority, has more power or knowledge, than the other.

Let me illustrate how the inequality works. In the *client – therapist* dynamic, you need the therapist to get your fix. The therapist is there to guide you and help you. There is much in the training of therapists that contribute to this distancing, keeping control, not letting the client see you as a person. There is a belief that if the client sees you at a course going through your own process, they can lose faith in your ability. It would take you off their pedestal, so to speak.

With the *disciple – guru*, it's the guru who has the power and the information. The disciple is expected to be obedient and faithfully carry out all instructions without question. It's not exactly rocket science to point out that the potential for abuse of such absolute power is real and there.

The *pupil – teacher* is yet another dynamic where power over is much more the rule than empowerment. The pupil is expected to learn what the teacher teaches and give the teacher's answer on tests. Rarely are students expected or encouraged to think independently and give answers outside the box. A friend of mine just completed an advanced course at university, where the final exam was a research paper. The sources she was allowed to quote from were very limited and narrow in scope.

The *child – parent* dynamic is an obvious one, where it's the parent who exercises control, makes decisions and has the power. How often don't parents push their children to have opportunities they didn't have and so on, without stopping to consider what is in the best interest for the child.

The *lover – healer*, what do I mean by that? It's when you get together with another, but you feel they need help or fixing. What you are saying is you don't like them the way they are. You come into the relationship so you can help them get well or get over a hurt or whatever. You make them dependent on you. They are not going to thank you for it and they will not stay around out of gratitude. When they do figure out your game they will leave with resentment in their hearts. Like everyone, all they want is to be loved, for who they are, right now.

And that is the dilemma with all these relationships. The implication is that you are not all right the way you are in this very moment. That some improvement is needed before you become acceptable and lovable. In the new world, these kinds of relationships can no longer exist. We have to stop giving our power away to someone else, to something outside ourselves.

By putting another on a pedestal, we are not really seeing them. By giving more credence to another than we do ourselves, we belittle ourselves in the process. When someone else is your authority, you don't believe in yourself. If you feel a need to be an authority, you are putting yourself above others. Is this what you want?

The best therapy sessions I've had have been when I have traded as an equal with another therapist. The best learning comes from freely sharing what I know with another and making a new rich mix. I truly believe we need to get away from the unequal way of doing relationships we have now. We need to let go of winning and losing, of being right or wrong, of thinking "either or" instead of "and." It's time to pitch control, manipulation and power-over out the window and let in the fresh breezes of empowerment.

It used to be that we read books by established authorities. That is changing. There is a whole new genre emerging called reality, where we read real life stories, by ordinary people who have gone through life changing experiences. This is good. We are moving from a select few having the answers to people like you and me sharing our experience, insight and learning with each other. There is a great equalization happening across the world. Internet is helping change this, it is no longer possible to keep the lid on, to lie to the people. The internet is truly power to the people. Yes, indeed!

These are my opinions

Please keep in mind that these are my opinions. I do not expect you to share them. I do not expect you to agree with me. I do hope to stimulate your thinking. I want you to have your own thoughts. To have your own opinions. To have your own feelings.

I believe in diversity. When we share our thoughts and dialogue about ideas, we can together create a new world. Where everyone is valued. Where we respect each other. One of my pet peeves is being sold someone else's idea of salvation. Just because you love a product doesn't mean it is right for me. Telling me about it is great, insisting I have to have it is not.

So keep in mind that these are my opinions. Read and ponder and sort. Take what works for you and leave the rest.

Eighteen

Results or characteristics?

When I interviewed with Swedish companies for project management and logistics positions, I frequently ended up at a personnel consultant for a battery of tests. It is standard practice to test interesting applicants for personality characteristics. Because of the results shown on my resume, they were interested in me. My achievements were, to say the least, above average. Then the personnel consultant took a look and came back with, "she does not fit the profile you are looking for." To clarify, I was interviewing for management positions in heavy industry, positions that were not traditionally filled by women. You may find this surprising, I did. How can a country where such a high percentage of the women work and the education level is so high, not have women managers? Certainly there were women engineers, in a higher proportion than in other countries. Part of the answer lies in the liberal maternity leave, part of it lies in tradition. It is assumed that women will have children, therefore they are not considered for the heavy management jobs in industry. Unlike in politics and the service sector, where women are well represented.

The assumption in heavy industry is that to be successful, you need to be assertive, almost on the verge of aggressive. I was told more than once that to be able to "pound my fist on the table" as the Swedish expression goes, was a prerequisite for getting a job as far as they were concerned. It seemed to be of no consequence to them that I had achieved far better results than the "table-pounders" they traditionally hired. As they had not seen women in these roles, they could not fathom how I would cope in them. I would point out that the job I was interviewing for was essentially the same as I'd had in the United States, and I had done just fine, thank you. They couldn't see it.

Sweden has a very high immigration rate. Statistically, it has one of the worst track records of assimilating its immigrants into the work force and society. The people who come here are for the most part highly educated and skilled professionals like engineers and medical doctors. I can see how difficult it is. I'm Swedish and I can't get a job here, because I don't have Swedish experience, I don't think like a Swede (thank God and thanks to thirty years of Americanization), and I didn't go to University here. If I had they would "know" me. I'm considered too foreign to fit in.

One of the main problems in organizations is that we tend to look for people to fit predetermined boxes, characteristics, education and experience, instead of looking at results and how one goes about achieving them. If we would think about it with more flexibility, we would have better organizations and get better results. Thinking outside the box, taking a chance on someone you may not normally hire, whether they are "over-qualified" or lack experience, or comes from a different background, can give you far greater gains than you imagine. You have to risk in order to grow. If we always go for the safe bet, we wouldn't have any new inventions, we would not progress.

Organizational dilemmas

The organizational dilemma for inventors is a big one. When you start a new venture, you don't know how to set it up for optimal functioning. You may be good at product development and sales, but weak in production or logistics. You may be really excellent at inventing and sorting details, but not know how to market your product. I've known several inventors and I can see that it's hard to know how to structure the venture from the start. After a few years, with experience and know-how gained along the way, it's a lot clearer. Being able to renegotiate contracts and organizational structure is imperative when you start something new.

Ask yourself, if I were starting this organization from scratch, how would I structure it? What role(s) would I want to fill? How do I want to set up my interaction with others? These are important questions for any venture, and apply equally to big organizations and romantic partnerships. Organizations need diversity. If we both think alike, one of us is unnecessary. An important point to consider in company structures or networks is who leads and who follows. If you need to lead, make sure you are structurally in a leadership position. Back seat driving never works and is impossible to implement. At Scott Paper we used to talk about making sure the tail doesn't wag the dog whenever we had project teams made up of employees from several departments. It was critical to the project's success that the project leader represented the key discipline, or you ended up with the tail wagging the dog.

There has been hoards written about vision statements in other books and I won't try to do it justice here. In chapter five I talked about puzzle pieces as a metaphor for vision. Where are you going and what is it you see when you get there? You will find the companion exercise at the end of Chapter twenty-three. Use it as an exercise in vision statement, if you wish.

From control to networks

There are many examples of traditional organizations based on control and rigid procedures. One obvious one is the Swedish social security administration, where everything is organized to follow a set routine. Heaven help you if you ask for something where they have no procedure to follow. I needed a statement for the IRS that I pay social taxes in Sweden. There is no form for that. They could not fulfill my simple request. This kind of bureaucratic government agency exists everywhere. They seem bent on not allowing people to think for themselves or in any way encourage a problem-solving attitude.

Lest you think the rigid organizations only exist in the government sphere, think again. I recently tried to do business with a new age distributor of books. They were as hard to get in with as Fort Knox. Makes me wonder how long they will be in business.

My original publisher is a new type of company. Using modern print-on-demand technology and the power of the internet, they are poised to change the nature of the publishing industry. Instead of editors deciding what will be available to read, the buying public decides. Anyone can publish and it becomes very democratic what is sold. Traditional self-publishing houses have focused on selling the production package. Author services companies work with the authors to make sure that those who want to be successful have all the tools and help they need and want to market, distribute, sell and promote their books.

Traditional publishing houses will be around for a long time I'm sure. The access they have to distribution channels is considerable and their marketing can't be beat. Yet of all the books written, they can only publish a few. Instead of still focusing on getting my first book published traditionally, I'm now writing my third book. I have grown enormously and I can see that my writing has improved a lot. Many times the really good book comes after we've been writing a while. How many people write a best seller the first time out? Not many.

Another inkling of the network structure of the future can be seen with Vedic Art. It has no membership lists and no requirements. The principles are taught, groups come together, and teachers are trained. There are no dues. If you wish to subscribe to their email news you may. If you are trained as a teacher, you may ask to be listed on the Vedic Art website. Information is spread by word of mouth. There is no advertising or traditional marketing. It is simple. It is a network of people who share an interest in painting from inside out, coming from the place of *I am*. The network is not restricted by national boundaries or political affiliations. It is free.

I see evidence that we will have more and more of these loose networks. We join together for a common cause or interest, we share experience and thoughts, we exchange, we work together, for a short or long time, across the globe. The internet is an important tool in this transformation.

When the Shen therapy organization split, I had hoped a network would form, of therapists who shared an interest in emotional healing, biofield therapeutics and related topics. Such a network would enable a cross pollenization of thoughts and experiences from Rosen, Gestalt, Journey, Shen, Kairos, hypnotherapy, NLP and many more. I believe such diverse networks would move healing further along than the current focus on narrow organizational disciplines. From my own experience of trading with a very diverse mix of therapists I must say it's been of more value than simply trading with those trained like me.

Nineteen

Setting limits

This week has been a theme of letting go, of cleaning out the old so the new can come in. Tomorrow is spring equinox so I've been cleaning on the physical, as well as in my life.

I've been very good as supporting others, including them in activities, writing about other events in my newsletters and recommending other therapists and courses. They have taken so much space there wasn't much left for me. Time for a change. Focus on me. The last newsletter I sent out I focused on just me. No news about global meditations or my friends' courses. Just me.

I have a friend who has been chewing on the same problem for a very long time. She tackles one and another pops up - but it's always the same theme. She says it never seems to end and she never seems to get to the stuff she really wants to do. I've tried being supportive, encouraging her to let the emotions out, offering help with the solution. And I know I'm not the only one who questions what she is doing. You know how it's always easier to see someone else's problem. I too have issues that I chew on, and then I get sick of myself and find a way to shift the focus or do something more constructive with my time.

I wanted to find a better way to say to my friend, "I don't want to listen to the same issue over and over." It seems no matter what I say, she just keeps going. Ok, it's not my job to fix her, but as I get to spend time with her I need to have a tool that works to shift the focus. I'm sure you've all been or are in situations where it's not possible to remove yourself from the situation. It may be a colleague or a close relative.

I remember the first time I used the phrase, "you've told me this several times before, is there something new you want to tell me about it?" The person hung up on me. Then our relationship changed and I no longer had to listen to long harangues. Setting limits. Learning to set limits in a good way. We don't help another by standing there and letting them go on and on ad nauseum. All they are doing is feeding the problem, giving energy to their misery. I don't want to waste my life energy listening to it and I hope my friends tell me to shut up if I chew and stew over the same thing without making progress.

I do believe we need to experience the problem emotionally, to really let the hurt out, feeling it deep in our cells and expressing our feelings. Then let it go, do something else and eventually new solutions pop in.

Yes, I know, it's easier said than done. Letting go is one of the hardest skills to learn. But necessary and essential.

A friend shared with me a gentle approach to stop course participants from taking up all the air space in a sharing circle. In her shamanic training, there was a woman who did just that. The leader gently stopped her and said, "I'm going to give you something you probably have never had - a limit." Learning to set boundaries is part of our earth plane lessons. Sometimes you have to be rude to get the message across. After all, who is the most important person in your life?

Anger

At least one therapy school teaches that anger is a secondary emotion. What they are saying is that anger covers another emotion; like hurt or guilt or fear. I agree that can be the case. But then there is pure anger. Right use of anger can be very healing, in setting limits, being true to our emotions and ourselves. Some people believe it's not spiritual to be angry. I believe that all emotions have to be allowed, not just the sweet ones.

Ok, we need to be cognizant and not just spew old anger out all over the place, but for those of us who were brought up to be nice girls, learning how to let it rip can be very freeing. Not letting it out will make you sick and if you hold it in because of consideration for the other person, you may do more damage to yourself in the long run. I'm clear as a bell that letting it rip won't resolve it with the other party, but it may save your sanity. Just don't expect to be understood.

I notice that my friends who let their emotions fly and who also are ok with their friends losing control, seem to have much healthier relationships. I too feel more comfortable being out of control when I'm with them. I don't think it's healthy to always have to think about how you should act responsibly. So if you feel inhibited in letting it fly, that may be just the thing you need to allow yourself to do. Conversely, if you have no restraint, check out the other side for a while.

I used to think I had no anger. I never felt angry, I smiled most of the time. But lots of people would get angry with me, and the level of unloading was pretty vicious. In therapy, I discovered I had tons of anger, murderous anger and rage that had never been allowed to be expressed. Freeing all that energy up lifted my chronic fatigue, normalized my low blood pressure and eliminated the low blood sugar or hypoglycemia I had been troubled with for years.

Who am I?

I seem to be going through an identity crisis. Who I thought I was, what I have identified myself with, may no longer be true. I question everything. I wrote two books, does that make me a writer? I paint and people tell me I have talent, does that make me a painter or an artist? I did career and for a long time that was my identity. I only recently uncovered the deep hurt when I was let go from my job and career. I had poured my soul into my work and it wasn't of value? Gee, that hurt. A lot.

And sending the letter to my male friend, I don't know what we are about but let's find out. So who am I then? If sex is not on the agenda, then what do we do? I find that even scarier. I know and feel comfortable in the role where we feel attraction and jump into bed together. But is that my identity and if I take that away then who am I?

I was lying in bed pondering this. I think I am a planner and organizer. I have prided myself on being really good at it. What if that isn't who I am?

I've always claimed I can only be interested in one man at a time. I am monogamous. What if that isn't true?

I realize all the assumptions, rules and mental constructs only limit me to being present in the now.

I do the experience, but it's not my identity. When I paint or dance I become the process. I think I am being trained to live life in that way. I am the love and the life energy. I do the roles, but they aren't my identity. In doing the Play with Possibilities group I was free to try and experiment because I had no ego tied up in proving that I was a good leader or facilitator. Well, maybe just a tad. Of course I was pleased when people liked what I had done.

Letting ourselves fail, to experiment, to live life without attachment to the outcome. To risk, to grow.

I have always thought of myself as not competitive. What if that isn't true either? I can see all these limits I have swallowed as part of enculturation and taking on standard beliefs. Having lived in different countries with different norms and attitudes has helped to loosen my thinking, to loosen a chink in the armor. Boy do we need it! We have no idea how rigid our thought patterns are and how automatic our assumptions are about things.

Giving myself permission to not have sex, to let go of the assumption that sex is a part of the get together with a man, has freed me up immensely. I don't have to know what it's about. I am free to let them show interest in me and I don't have to please them.

In pondering what I really want and stating that clearly, I felt very confused. What do I want? Where am I going and why? What do I do when I get there? What is the Divine plan? What comes, is that I can only decide in the now what I feel is right and follow that thread. I may write today, paint tomorrow, do nothing the next day, look for a job the next, co-teach a course the next, be a wife the next, or lover or whatever. It's time to let the logical structured mind go on vacation, the one who needs to control and decide, and just be. It's time to let go of having an identity.

Instead of presenting myself as a writer, I say I have written two books. Whenever I speak to someone I don't have to drag all my past into it. I can be present here and now and deal with what is here. This last weekend a few of my friends joined the painting group I have been part of for several years. We have been the same constellation since our startup, so in a way it was a big deal to take in new blood. But they fit right in. All three newcomers said they felt like they had already been part of the group for a long time. On the way home I suggested that in the fall perhaps we could form our own group locally. "No we like this group," they responded in unison. Fall is a long way off. I have a habit of projecting into the future, seeing possibilities. At times it takes me out of being here and now and doing the experience that is happening now.

And that's another thing. I take responsibility for making sure stuff happens. I organize groups, I call around, I include everyone and I pass information along. Sure it's nice, but nobody pays me to do this. I need to get clear on when I do it because I really want to and when I do it out of habit. I seem to want to create something that lasts, but it seldom works out that way. A great way for the universe to teach me to be here and now. That life is change.

I friend of mine got married, again. This was a few years ago. She was really skittish. What if it didn't work out? She had already been married two or three times and they hadn't worked out. Why do we assume that just because a marriage ends that "it didn't work out?" Why can't we look at it in the true context - we were done. We came together and had the experience we were meant to have and now it's time to move on. Anyway, my friend's spouse to be said "would it be easier if you thought of it as *I may get married a hundred times*?" That did it! She could see the ludicrous in limiting herself to the number of experiences.

We have so many judgments of this is good and that is bad. It used to be that having a job for life was good. We've had to toss that idea out the window. I think the same is happening with everything in the world. Piece by piece all our old assumptions, behavior patterns and identities are being put to the test. The old structures that no longer serve us are coming apart at the seam. And it is good.

So who am I? Good question. It's time to crawl back into bed at 5am.

Cornucopia

A month ago I bought the Statue of Liberty charm for my bracelet. I like to think of the symbol as *the Goddess of Freedom,* as she is known in Swedish. Sure enough, issues about freedom have surfaced and percolated and rearranged my outlook. Last weekend I bought another charm - *Cornucopia* - abundance, flow, riches...

And the issues come flying in - one of the responses to my Paint without Purpose course came from a contact in Ottawa. He offered to help scout out book signing opportunities for me. This morning I was reflecting on that and how nice it felt to be supported. One of my things is *cooperation and mutual support.* But mostly it's me that cooperates and supports and I truly have had very little experience of being supported. What's become clear lately is how much I show up for others, take charge of arrangements, make contact, bring information, recommend people. I'm not saying I shouldn't do those things but I've been putting it in a new perspective. It's not a given that it's up to me to organize things. For example if our painting group wants to do an exhibition or go on an art tour to Berlin, it's not necessarily me that needs to make sure it happens. I can toss out the idea and if it's worth doing someone else will get on the bandwagon with me. Typically I toss out an idea then proceed to take care of all the details. I don't have to do that. I can sit back and relax and only pick up what I truly want to do. I don't have to be so accomplished and organized.

Back to my Ottawa friend. It brought up tears of not having been supported in the past. Of how much energy it takes to do everything on my own, how exhausting it is to be the driving force and not really get any help. As my tears bubbled through, I thought of a conversation I had with my brother's sister-in-law. She was telling me how she helped my brother get a job back in their hometown. She went to bat for him. She had gone to High School with the owner of the company and used that connection to ask him to seriously consider my brother, even though he was "overqualified." Now that's support. And it makes me sad that I haven't had that kind of support. It's always up to me alone to make connections. It makes me very sad. Correction – it has been true in the past, up to now.

And again how when I lost my job I lost my income, and how much I miss having an income (Cornucopia at work). I miss being a part of a larger context and I miss having an income that supports me. I miss having support. The other night I was talking to another friend who also has done a lot of women firsts. Now she wouldn't mind being a Mrs. and being supported, in an independent way of course. I have no idea what it would be like to be taken care of. I suspect I would like it. I like being doted on.

After starting the group Play with Possibilities I talked to several people who would have been interested in coming, but only to get, for free, without giving anything in return. They felt that one shouldn't have to pay for courses. Part of the Swedish mentality and system. What it brought up for me is I want to get paid. I no longer am willing to do it for free. It's quite a shift in my perspective and attitude. I am no longer willing to let people take advantage of me.

I know it's a popular belief in the new age community that one should do what one loves and do it for free and that will lead you to abundance. I believe we should do what we love and if in our hearts we want to give it for free then it's appropriate. We also don't need to be doormats. We can stand up for ourselves in the marketplace of life and demand to be paid what we are worth.

Perhaps the trick in networking and support is to find the mates who operate on the same principles as you do. Where there truly is support and exchange. We help each other. We aren't only in it for what it can do for me. My connection in Ottawa may have help of some of my contacts. So often I have helped people with information and connections, then after awhile I realize it's been a one-way street. The energy exchange is rarely 50/50 but if one is always giving or providing and not being fed in return then it's time to make a spring cleaning of the network connections.

Pondering Cornucopia, I now want to make money, to be a part of life, to participate and to be paid well. I am no longer content to sit at the sidelines and be a spectator. I want my money and I want it now. I want a more affluent lifestyle. That wasn't my wish when I moved here to my little house in the country. I almost felt guilty when I went to the Create your Future seminars and my wish was so basic, others were putting goals out there for big material things and big jobs and on and on. But we go through different stages in our lives. I've done the heavy duty career I've done the contemplate the inner worlds, now I want the freedom to travel, income, something bigger to do, companionship and live in the flow. I want what God wants for me. I believe God wants us to be happy and live rich lives - materially, emotionally, physically and spiritually - that is the Divine Design.

Twenty

My beliefs are not your beliefs

I've had several run-ins with friends over beliefs about relationships. Because the material triggered has had such a strong emotional charge, my friends have unwittingly tried to impose their beliefs on me. Why can't we accept that people have different viewpoints?

I quite openly state I want a man. What's so odd about that, except we don't usually state it so clearly? We tend not to say it at all, keeping our hopes quiet. Well, if I were unemployed no one would think it strange if I say I want a job. But being honest about wanting a man seems to scare people.

Anyway I had this man friend who potentially could be a lover, a relationship, a colleague, a therapy connection and/or a friend. At the moment he has a girlfriend and he and I are friends. We chat for hours about everything, not very often, but when we do we seem to cover a lot of ground. One woman friend in particular had trouble getting her head around me being friends with a man I was interested in beyond friendship. She was horrified that I had laid my cards on the table and told him I was interested. Well why not? Nothing ventured, nothing gained.

She kept ragging on me about not getting my hopes up, and she wondered if I was really meant to have a relationship at all. It seemed to her I was meant to be independent. Well to me relationship does not mean that you have to give up who you are. On the contrary, I believe that the more you are yourself the more love can flourish.

Ok, so here is my woman friend with all her fears and beliefs percolating about relationships. Instead of having a dialogue about the beliefs and emotions stirred, she imposes her beliefs on me, not realizing it's her beliefs but thinking it is how things should be.

How often don't we do that? We assume we have the truth with a capital T and insist that others also adopt our solution. It's another form of emotional pollution.

Interference and sabotage

When fears are stirred and jealousy rears it ugly head it's not unusual for interference and sabotage to occur. It may or may not be conscious. Your well-meaning family or friends tell you that the man you are interested in, "doesn't see you that way, dear." Or they don't tell you he called. Or they tell him that you have someone else. The scenarios are endless and can really get in the way.

Up until quite recently I had assumed that when someone unloads on you, they are coming from the unhealed part of themselves, but that deep down they don't mean to hurt you. I've had to revise my understanding. In healing sessions I have gone back and been confronted with the painful truth that they did know what they were doing and yes they wanted to hurt me. It's hard to accept that deep down the person you were with really hated you. They only pretended to love you so they could manipulate and torture you. Some of them were jealous and some of them just wanted to make me hurt, out of spite and hate. It's a really yucky place to be, and it did not feel good to go there.

One workshop I was at, there was a woman who shared that she enjoyed hurting people. At the time I felt horrified. Now I must say I admire her courage and honesty in telling the truth. By admitting to herself and openly talking about it to others she began the healing journey. You can't heal what you won't let yourself look at or admit.

Another issue I hadn't been able to release was trusting my own intuition. I would sense one thing and the other person would say it is not so. I hadn't wanted to look at that they were deliberately lying, for their own gains. They weren't interested in the truth. It's hard enough to be lied to, it's a painful realization to be lied to by people who say they care for you. Love and lying don't go together. Lies come from fear.

What is really going on?

Continuing the theme of interference from well meaning friends, I am reminded of another incident. I was traveling with a woman friend of mine and we had stopped for lunch. As we were sitting outside perusing the menu, a car pulls up and out pours four young bucks. One of them catches my attention, big time. He is absolutely gorgeous, to me anyway, and he exudes a strong presence, sensual and sexual. Lots of life energy percolating there. I say to my friend, "I like the guy in the striped shirt." She says, "not me, he scares me." She makes it very clear she wants nothing to do with these guys. She even has us trade places with some excuse that the smoke from my cigarette is bothering her, so I can't see the guys, I now sit with my back to them.

While we eat we can hear them talking, but can't quite make out the language. They're obviously checking us out but my friend is so making clear she wants none of their attention. After the meal I go inside to the restroom. When I come back out I discover my friend is chatting up a storm with the guy I expressed interest in. What in the world is going on here?

First she says I want nothing to do with them, and then she starts up a conversation. I'm confused. Before leaving, we chat with them some, they want us to come with them down the coast. My friend is adamant she is not interested.

Well in hindsight I can see several explanations. My friend is jealous and she wants to keep me for herself. She may be scared to get involved with the boys. Or she wants him for herself. Either way, her fears stop me from pursuing what I really want. Somehow I have made her needs greater than mine, I let her needs rule. If I had been true to myself, I would have stayed in my seat, struck up a conversation and maybe gone off with the boys. If my girlfriend didn't want to we should have split up and gone our separate ways.

Was her motivation to control me or to do what was best for her or me? It's hard to say in hindsight, but there were other times with her that she acted jealous if other people got too much of my attention. So when a man walked in that really caught my attention, it scared her.

Another time, another girlfriend. We both worked at the same place. She was telling me she'd been talking to this guy, nice looking fellow, neither one of us knew him very well, but he worked at the same place too. When he found out she knew me, he'd exclaimed, "she's a fox." Nice to know he might be interested in me. I thought nothing more of it until my girlfriend called me a few weeks later. "Guess who I went home with and spent the night with?" she says. "I have no idea," I reply, "who?" Yeah, you guessed it, the guy who thought I was a fox. She just had to have him because he was interested in me, not because she really liked him. To this day I can't fathom what goes on in someone's mind who seduces someone just to show off. I guess I operate differently.

With friends like that who needs enemies? Needless to say she is no longer a friend of mine.

I know it happens that a mate falls in love with a best friend. If it's out of love I can accept it. Yes it's going to hurt in the short run, but if it's true love you can't deny it. But there is a big difference when you talk about seduction, going for someone because you have to have him or her, then it's about manipulation and control and has absolutely nothing to do with love.

Earlier I described how another friend had been ragging on me for so easily going to bed with guys. When I think about it, most of them were men I knew through work or friends, in other words it wasn't like I was picking up total strangers. My friend who said this, used to pick up men, total strangers, when she would be away on vacation. I find that much harder to understand, how do you just go off with a total stranger, then find my behavior odd. As sexually active as I've been there have always been more dimensions to it. The few times I've picked up perfect strangers have taught me that *I've never found anything in a bar worth keeping.*

Dealing with imposed beliefs

As I sat this morning with my cup of tea I pondered the numerous times friends have ragged on me about how I should be. Or rather, they tell me I'm wrong, that I need to change or that I need to be realistic. Well Eva, turn it around, I heard my Higher Self prod. Turn it around? I thought, what does that mean?

First of all, turn it around. Instead of swallowing their assumption that you are wrong, assume that what you are doing is actually right - for you. This is the important distinction. It is right for you. Obviously whatever you are doing is something that is not ok for the other person to do. They are ragging on you for things they fear or do not allow themselves to be or do.

It is their fears and limitations. They have no business imposing them on you. However I believe we get these criticisms so we can get stronger in our resolve to be ourselves, to be true to ourselves. If we never encountered resistance we would not get strong. Resistance actually helps us grow.

I believe you are always more in tune with your Higher Self than anyone else can be. You know deep in your heart what is true. But with all the interference most of us get, we have long since quit trusting our own inner knowing.

So when my friends were ragging on me about relationships, they were really talking about their own beliefs.

Better late than never

A friend loaned me a book, because she wanted me to do a past life regression on her. She had read Sylvia Browne's *Past Lives, Future Healing* and wondered if I could use the script from the book? I had worked with my friend in the past, and she wanted someone there with her who wouldn't back off when the really good stuff came bubbling up. Nice recommendation. If you've read my other books, you already know how strongly I feel about poking around in someone else's psyche without proper training and experience.

I read the book with interest. The regression script was different than the ones I had learned in my hypnotherapy training and I liked Sylvia's approach even better. I wanted to test it for myself, so I made a recording of the script. By now I have done so much of this kind of work on myself that I feel safe in doing it on my own. If you are a beginner, get someone you really trust and who has appropriate experience to work with you. I would not recommend you do this on your own if you are a novice.

As I recorded the script, I noticed there were places where my voice choked up and I had to pause the tape. When I laid down to listen to it, the memories were clear and the emotions were strong. This method takes you straight to the source of your problems. The story that unfolded explained a whole lot that I had not been able to break through any other way.

The year was 1721, I was a young girl of seventeen named Anja, in Brussels. My hair was long, I was dressed in a white dress and wore a wreath on my head. I was with the man I loved, my intended, and I was pregnant with his child. We loved each other very much and were excited about our love child. When we went to tell my father of our plans to get married, all hell broke loose. My father in that life made sure to separate us and got my love sent off where we couldn't contact each other. My father lied and schemed to make sure we never saw each other again. He also made sure to brain wash me that the man I loved really hadn't loved me, it had all been in my head that he was at all interested in me. The child I carried died and I ended my days as a prostitute in Amsterdam.

It was to say the least a very powerful regression. The people in that life were people I know in this life. So much fell into place. So much healing is taking place.

The child I lost has been working with me from the other side to help me release the grief and loss. She explained why she opted out, less than a year old. She did it so I could be free of the father who hated me. Thank you Belinda!

I have been working through the pain of being betrayed by my father in that life. Realizing that he did not want what was best for me. He lied so well I lost touch with my own inner knowing. I've had a major issue in trusting my intuition and seeing people as they really are. Thank God I have now recovered that sense of inner knowing.

Another core issue I've been working on is abandonment, or fear of abandonment. In that life I thought my love abandoned me. He didn't. He was as powerless as I was in preventing the father from destroying our lives. What really touches my heart is that I have been able to reconnect with the love we felt for each other in that life. We had everything going for us only to have it taken away by a vengeful and jealous parent.

Needless to say the father from 1721 is no longer in my life. Sure we need to heal and forgive, but how could I ever trust someone capable of that kind of treachery? That person has already done enough damage.

I feel free in a way I haven't before. Sure it would be nice to rekindle the love. After nearly three hundred years we are different people and we would have to start from "who are you now?" But it would be a much better base than most relationships are built on.

I am so grateful that the whole past life memory with all the emotions came up to be healed. It's been very painful but worth every tear. I highly recommend the regression Sylvia Browne uses in *Past Lives, Future Healing*.

Release through expression

One interesting thing that has been happening during the writing of this book is my body's reaction. In parts, it has been heavy and slow moving. The energy has felt lethargic. I have experienced pain, particularly in my hands and fingers, at other times in my arms or shoulders. I questioned if I should be writing when I felt stiff and in pain. As I reflected, I would realize I hadn't written for a few days, so the cause of the pain probably was not overusing my "typing tools."

So I sat down to write. Lo and behold, as the words unfolded on the page, as I spoke the heretofore unspoken, as I released what I had held inside, my pain went away. My hands became loose and free, my fingers no longer felt stiff. The pain in my arms left, the discomfort in my shoulders dissolved. I feel freed up. I wonder how many people are walking around with body pain that is caused by held in thoughts and emotions. Not expressing what is bubbling inside makes the pain chronic.

In my therapy training we were taught that to release the tension we needed to experience the emotion fully. I still believe that is true, that to get to the bottom of hurts we need to go into the pain. However, I notice how great the benefits have been from the expressive arts, like dancing, painting, toning and writing. I believe we need to do a variety of things to become whole. We can't get there solely through one method or by digging through the past.

To become whole we need to bring out what is inside of us. We have to risk going out on a limb, to express our inner selves, to share our gift with the world. What we hold inside is our salvation if we bring it out, if we lock it up inside ourselves it is our destruction. The energy must move and flow freely. It is why we are here – to dance in the energy of life.

Twenty-One

If you love something

Pay attention to how you feel about your friends. Do you want what is really best for them, even if it means losing them? I believe love is about freedom. When we truly love ourselves and other people we are free. We accept them as they are. Only first we have to find out who we are and who the other person is.

The lead-in to this book is one of my favorite sayings:

If you love something

set it free

if it comes back to you

it is yours

if it doesn't

it never was

Let's take a look at what that means. The hardest lesson in life is letting go. Many spiritual organizations use the saying *let go and let God*. Such simple, easy words, yet so hard to do.

When we fall in love, we want to keep that very special someone. The last thing in the world we want is to lose them. Unfortunately, the more we hang on, the more we control, the more likely we are to lose the very thing we cherish.

One of my friends was married for thirty years. Her husband was so afraid of losing her while they were married, that he wasn't free to be himself. Now that they are divorced, and he has "lost her" in the way he thought it must be, they are the best of friends. Ironically, he now treats her in the way she longed for while they were married. Now he brings her flowers, goes shopping with her, calls to see how she is and helps out in many ways. The way I see it, their relationship is now where it was meant to be all along. He lives in a cabin style house, where he can watch TV and sports to his hearts content. She lives in a nice apartment surrounded by pretty things where she can entertain with Royal Danish china and have her peace and quiet. Both of them seem quite content with the arrangement, now that they have let go of the encultured idea of how it should be. It goes to show that men and women can be friends.

If I meet a guy and I find him interesting, why would it matter if he were married or not? It doesn't make sense to me that I would only be interested in him if he is available. There are many ways we relate to others. Friendship is one of them. If I wouldn't want a man for a friend, I certainly wouldn't want him for a partner. We aren't used to thinking in those terms, but when it comes down to it, it's only natural.

Needing to control others destroys the free flow of energy in relationships and organizations. We control when we try to book the other one up months in advance, trying to make sure they are going to be with us, not giving them a chance to make other plans before we get to them.

We control when we get possessive, when we can't stand the thought of him or her going home to be alone, when we cry to get our way. We control when we call or write all the time, sending out insecurity signals, needing confirmation all the time.

We control when we play the guilt card, when we help someone out then expecting them to stay with us to return the favor. Being manipulated into doing something out of guilt always feels sticky and yucky.

Jealousy and envy are sure to put the kibosh on the free flow of love. If these feelings get stirred in you, go work them out through therapy or other means. These feelings are real and quite icky. We all get them, but if we use jealousy to get possessive of our partner, we are sure to lose him or her in the end. One ex used to accuse me of having affairs. The thought hadn't entered my mind. But it occurred to me that I might as well.

Letting go implies trust. One friend who lives apart from her husband for extended periods gets asked a lot about fears of infidelity. She says it can happen anywhere, you meet people all the time. The key when living apart is to trust and to have an open communication. You can't go worrying about what the other one is doing when you are not there. It's important to discuss rules or assumptions, but you need to give each other the freedom to be adults.

If we are honest, with ourselves, with each other, we can make things work. It's when we come from a need to win, to have, to possess and control, that we lose.

One man I was with insisted I cook for him to prove that I loved him. In his head, he was loved if the woman cooked for him. What has love got to do with insisting I be a certain way? There is nothing wrong with wishing or asking, but insisting kills any inclination you may have had to be of service.

There is a world of difference in stating a wish list and leaving it up to the other one to fulfill it or not, to demanding that they fulfill every one of your requirements whether they want to or not. Being expected to fulfill a demand has nothing to do with love.

Whatever it is, are you doing it out of love? One of my women friends is married to a man who loves target shooting. The competitions are not exactly what you would call an exciting spectator sport. But my friend goes to watch hubby compete. Why? Not because she has a burning interest in the sport, but she loves her husband that much. He doesn't demand that she do it. She goes because she wants to of her own free will.

Do you like your partner just the way they are? Or do you wish they would change? Do you work on "improving" them? Needing to have the other one change so you can love them isn't going to get you anywhere. Sure, we all have attributes that are less easy to love, but we need to learn to accept each other as we are. Most of all, we need to learn to accept ourselves. Contrary to what we have been brought up to believe, we are good enough, we are lovable, we are worthy and we are human, and therefore fallible.

Being human implies imperfection. How many of us experienced it being ok to fail, to make mistakes, to smudge that pretty dress, to spill on Mom's best tablecloths? Our parents had it even worse. They had much more pressure than we did, to behave, to do good, to live up to their parents' expectations. It's no wonder they passed on their rigid upbringing to us. They didn't know any better.

However there is hope. We can grow to love ourselves, and each other, in healthy ways. It seems the more I accept myself, and all my aspects, the more tolerant I become of others. If you feel intolerance, ask yourself what part of yourself you can't tolerate. You may be surprised at what you find.

Insisting on constant togetherness kills a relationship. We need time alone and with our other friends and interests. There isn't one of your friends who shares all your interests, not even the best of friends think and do alike. Why do we expect that a love relationship all of a sudden will fulfill all of our needs? I keep saying: discover where you intersect, enjoy where and when you meet, and let go of the rest.

Relationships

Relationships. A loaded word. Associations leap to romance. What we wish for and dream about. An assessment of what we actually have. But relationships are so much more. We have relationships at work, at home, with family, friends and lovers and most of all with ourselves.

I believe it is time to reassess our definition of relationships, to examine our values and longing, so we can redefine how to make relationships work in the world we now live in.

I believe it's time to discover who we really are. Get to know ourselves, and the other person. Really understand who we are and what we want, then find the areas where our interests and values intersect and let go of the rest. We need to transmute old patterns and beliefs and form new ways of relating to each other. To create meetings that are meaningful and meet our real needs. To quit trying to hammer other people as well as ourselves into structures that obviously aren't working. To free ourselves up to be who we were meant to be and give others the freedom to be themselves. Instead of trying to change other people, accept them as they are. To do that we first need to discover who they are. The same holds true for ourselves. We need to quit trying to make ourselves fit into a mold.

It's time to break old molds. Form new ways of relating that allow us to grow and develop. To set each other free.

Twenty-Two

Put yourself first

Last night I went to a concert with some of my painting friends. On the way home we were talking of setting limits and boundaries. Then a badger ran across the road right in front of my car. This morning I looked up the meaning of badger in the *Animal Speak* book:

> *Set limits, stand up for yourself. Let your emotions out. Your gift is to be determined.*

I did a creative dance session. Anger and frustration wanted out of my body. The importance of working with the physical body and really moving it is grossly underrated in traditional therapy circles. The dance helps the body get the stuff chugged loose, released, integrated and grounded. If you stop and think about it, dance is one of the most natural ways for us to be. Maybe therapeutically we would be better off if we looked at natural inclinations rather than get so academic about it.

In my morning meditation I went deeper into the issues and questions that are up for me at the moment. I was reminded of how my colleague and I would work through issues that we triggered in each other. In one instance I had just raised my rates, after calculating what I needed to charge to make a business out of my practice. She asks me, "how much will you now charge?" When I replied, her immediate reaction was, "I would never pay that!" I felt a twinge of fear in my stomach, and realized in an instant that this was her stuff. I told her so. She agreed, "yes, it is my own fear of being worth that much, I wouldn't be able to charge that sum." Both of us handled the fears in an adult fashion, we could talk about it and take the fears to the therapy table.

Most often in life, we don't get to deal with triggered emotions in such an adult manner. I also realize that I bend over backwards to deal with others responsibly and in an adult manner, even when their behavior is childish. I don't allow myself to fly off the handle, to take the whole bucket of hurt and spew it out, not stopping to worry about where it comes from or who it belongs to. But what if the most appropriate response would be to do just that, when someone else comes flying at you out of nowhere?

What if I reacted like a child? They are acting like a child. Perhaps this is the level it should be resolved at? My Higher Self suggested in morning meditation I write an open letter to all the people who have acted childishly toward me, and to let myself say what I am thinking, but too polite to say. So here goes.

Open letter to immature behavior

I have tried to respond to you like an adult. I haven't said what I really think about your behavior. It's time to let it out and let you have it. You don't seem to have any restraint in letting me have it so why should I be so darn responsible and polite and mature. You don't seem to understand mature anyway and in my trying to stay mature and polite I swallow what I need to say and I take on the guilt, that somehow it's all my fault and responsibility.

Grow up and quit projecting your crap onto me and others. Take responsibility for your actions and for God's sake, pause before you let that diarrhea of the mouth take off. I haven't asked for your opinion and what makes you think you have the answers for my life? What have you tied up in making me so wrong, why do you feel such a need to control me? I can make my own decisions thank you and I am willing to make mistakes. I do not want to be owned.

I haven't wanted to see that you really don't want what is best for me. You are selfish in the worst way. You think that by owning and steering me, you can gain something. No you have to get it for your self. I am tired of having you as a slug, sucking my energy. Grow up and behave like a mature adult. Take responsibility for your actions. If you find that people get angry with you, ask yourself what anger you hold within. Turn the flashlight back on yourself.

Why do you not wish me happiness? What is it that scares you so much with me taking on my power, with me taking space? Is it that you will no longer be able to live off my energy? You can no longer suck my life energy, you have to get your own. I am not going to allow it any longer. I am sick and tired of people who want to live their lives off of me, to get your kicks by hearing about all my excitement.

Sure I like company, but there are responsibilities that go along. I will not let you treat me however you want. If something I do or think scares you, say so. Don't just let it fly out of your mouth, like you have no control. You can exercise control. You can pause and think, before you just let loose with a stream of crap. Ask yourself why and what your motivation is in saying what you are saying. Do you really want what is best for me? Or are you letting fear, anger, jealousy rule your tongue?

Think before you speak. I do. It means I end up holding back, apparently too much. It has been to my detriment. But I know how unpleasant it is to be hit with a barrage of crap and I really don't want to do that to you. Do unto others.

What I haven't done is set limits when I should have. I have heard your crap without shouting STOP. I have sat there and listened and not been able to make sense of it. Of course I can't make sense of it. The whole litany is your unhealed inner garbage. It doesn't make sense. It's emotional pollution. It's garbage.

So when I finally do set limits, I try to be succinct and stick to the present. I don't want to heap the whole bucket on you. But you know what? This isn't just about me. It isn't just me that needs to look at what is going on. You have a responsibility too. Take a look at what triggered you. What was it I said or did that made your emotions go flying so the words spilled out of your mouth without restraint, without reflection of what in the world you were doing.

What makes you so intent on polluting my environment with your emotional baggage? Because that is what it is. It is emotional pollution and I am not having any more of it.

Whenever you find yourself having to share your opinion, insisting on giving advice, what is your motive? Tell me that. Why? I try not to impose my beliefs on you. I deserve the same respect. If you are afraid of stepping into your power, of sex, of fame, of fortune, whatever your fear is, please work it out. And don't try to make your fears and limitations mine. I won't buy them. You can't hold on to me by limiting me. I am free. You are free. Let go of your blocks. I'm letting go of mine.

It's time I quit thinking that you know more than I do. I have worked very hard on myself. I have come a long way. I know I don't have all the answers. But it's time that I quit assuming that it's me that has to change. That it's me that has to work through stuff. Just maybe it's you that has a problem and just maybe it's you that has a much deeper issue than I. It's time I quit letting people distract me and disturb and stop me from walking my divine path. So there!

Phew. That felt really good. I had no trouble at all letting the words flow. I needed to get all that off my chest. Which leads me to the next topic.

Turn it around

What if you turn it around? Let's look at some hypothetical examples. Let's say you get criticized over and over for being too meticulous. What if, instead of thinking you have to fix your problem, instead of thinking there is something wrong with being meticulous, you turned it around? Allowed yourself to think, this is right with me, being meticulous is my gift to the world.

What if you get ragged on about being a dreamer? You get told over and over to come down to earth and be realistic. If you turn it around, it becomes a gift instead of a burden. Instead of it being something wrong with you, it is what is right about you.

When others disapprove of your behavior, instead of thinking you have to change, let yourself turn it around. The behavior you are being chided for is perhaps what is right with you.

You are who you are. The way you were put together by God is how you were meant to be in order to fulfill your mission on earth. So let yourself stand tall with pride when the barrage comes. Know deep in your heart that what they are criticizing you for is what is right with you. Think about it, would Einstein have been able to achieve what he did if he had been "balanced?" So accept yourself as you are. All our skills and viewpoints are needed. God created us that way, so that there is a natural organization of skills and talents. Each and every one of us is needed.

Twenty-Three

Sacred space meditation

If you, like me, have worked on releasing emotions and projections ad nauseum, you may want some new tools. Here is a meditation exercise presented to me by my Higher Self to help sweep out the cobwebs of garbage in a different way.

Put out your do-not-disturb sign first, like turn off the phone, tell your housemates to leave you in peace and find yourself a private space. If your house is chaos, go sit in the car or go to the library. You can always find somewhere to be alone with yourself. I've meditated in bathrooms, in busy airports, on trains and once you get in the meditation habit you can do it anywhere. Use the outside distractions to take you deeper into yourself.

Now get yourself situated in meditation pose - sit up straight in a chair, on the floor in lotus position or lie down - whatever makes you comfortable. Then take a few deep breaths to center yourself, feel your body in the chair or against the floor. Ask your Higher Self to come in and help and be present with you during this exercise. Clarifying that you want help from your Higher Self keeps other astral helpers from showing up and mucking up the works.

Now take your attention into your sacral chakra. It's located in your belly about halfway between the top of your pubic bone and your navel. Bring your attention into your body so your focal point is in the center of your torso at the sacral chakra. Simply place your awareness at this point.

Keep your awareness on this sacral midpoint. If your attention wanders, it's ok. When you discover you've gone somewhere else, just bring your attention back to the sacral point. To begin with you may not feel much and only be aware of a point, or physical location in your body.

Then you may notice that the space expands, becomes light, you can palpate and feel the inner sanctum in you. As the light gets stronger, increase your focus, feel the light grow and expand. As the light gets stronger and expands it will push out of the way any remnants of negativity. You can look at it as an energy affirmation. It's also a nice break from all the digging and clearing and hard work. And it works.

Balance

After doing this meditation for about a week the rest of my body spoke up. Need for balance here, as I reached for an aquamarine necklace. Time to focus on the soul point, between the heart and throat chakras. I perceive the colors as purple and aquamarine here and as I focus on the point I sense a lightness and expansiveness in my chest. These points are further explained in the hara meditation covered in my first book.

The awakening

You know how it is when you meet someone new who really tickles your fancy. You get excited, you feel like you could kiss the world, you feel wonderful and... your fantasies take off. You see yourself with this mate, and your dream in your heart, your script goes playing in your mind. We all do this. We carry within us a puzzle picture of what we really want and when we meet that special someone all our fantasies rev up and get into high gear. Now the rub is that your mate has his own scenario, his own dreams, and his own idea of heaven. Reality soon comes crashing in when we discover the other person doesn't act according to our script. Boo-hoo!

Remember I wrote about puzzle pieces early on in this book? It's time to get back to doing some exercises around it. If we can identify our own end vision, our own idea of what the puzzle is supposed to look like, we become clearer in our intent. If the other people we are working with, whether a potential mate or members of a committee or colleagues at work, also can identify their end vision or puzzle picture, we will be miles ahead of the game.

Puzzle pieces exercise

Ground rule number one is to be totally honest with yourself. If what you want is not what your mate wants, now is the best time to find out so you can set each other free. If you don't, chances are you will spend your energies trying to get the other person to change, to conform to your dream. This is one of the major causes of friction between people. We can't seem to accept that others have different values and goals and lessons to do in this lifetime. Doesn't mean we can't love them, we just have to relate to them differently.

Ok, the exercise. Be honest with yourself. This exercise is situation specific, you need to focus on the mate or group you are currently with, and work from there. You can look at your life goals as well but there are many other ways to get that info.

This exercise works well for those who are visual. If that is not your style, then focus on what you would be hearing, or feeling, or sensing to get in touch with your puzzle vision.

Get yourself into a relaxed or meditative state, staring into space, in the hammock, on the couch or in your favorite chair. Now let your mind drift and daydream, let yourself float. Breathe easily and feel yourself get lighter and fuzzier in that logical brain of yours. Notice the clouds drifting by in the sky and let your mind go. Then with your mate or group in mind, let your mind show you images of what you carry inside as your dream, your vision. Rarely does it come as one complete "here I am" package, it comes more in bits and pieces, in wisps or floating images. But it'll be there.

Say you are a woman who's pondering a potential mate. What images come to mind? Do you see children trailing after him, do you see yourself making love in romantic settings, do you see yourself buying a house and fixing it up, a rich social life, sailing around the world, quiet evenings in front of the fireplace, or...

Let the images come and float through. Notice if there are other people involved and what activities you see yourself in, notice the role you put him in, what hopes and expectations you have of him in your dream.

The important thing here is to get in touch with your fantasy and be honest about it. Julia Roberts in the movie *Pretty Woman* told Richard Gere she wanted the fairy tale. She didn't want to be a kept woman, which he had offered her. It was painful to be honest as she thought she had lost him all together when she said, "no I want the fairy tale." In the movies we have to have happy endings so he came as the modern knight and rescued the princess out of the tower and she got her fairy tale ending. Just one example of letting go. You know

If you love something

set it free

if it comes back to you

it is yours

if it doesn't

it never was

When you come out of your drifty space and have let your fantasy roam, come back to the here and now and write down your images. You will see threads and common themes. Go ahead and dialogue with your mate or group about your true dreams, talk about what you think they really mean to you, be curious about the other people, try to understand them and their dreams. I think that is the true meaning of love, wanting to discover and know who the other person really is.

This exercise clarifies what you are really signing up for. Isn't the time to discover this now? Why wait until later and find out you thought you were signing up for something else entirely?

Twenty-Four

How do we meet people?

If the people you are meeting don't have dreams that match yours, perhaps you need to look in a different place. There are some common misconceptions about how we actually meet mates. I've been alone now for some time, and every once in a while my friends and I talk about going out dancing or to the pub to meet some men. But every time it falls flat, none of us have any interest in really going there anyway.

I've been working my way through the exercises in *Everyday Karma* by Carmen Harra. A key element in her work is to go through every single relationship you've ever had, it doesn't matter if they were short or long, you count them all and review the key elements of each one. I won't belabor them all here, as there were about fifty men to review, but I will share with you one statistic - how I met them all:

through work - 13

at school and hobbies - 14

through friends and colleagues - 19

going out - 4

Surprise, surprise the best way to meet people is to do life. When you focus on what you are interested in and participate in those activities, you naturally come in contact with others of like interest. These friends have other friends and so on.

Why not make your own tabulation of your relationships? Where did you meet? Was it by going out? Through school? At work? While engaged in a hobby? At a friend's house? Take a look at where and how you connect with people. Most often we meet through common interests and it is the rare exception where we pick someone up at a dance or other outing and the connection turns out to be a lasting one.

I related my research to a friend of mine. She confirmed my statistics and said there has been research done on this and the number one place we meet mates is through work. So there!

Then I talked to another friend of mine. When she reflected on how she had met the men in her life, it turned out she had met most of them by going out dancing. Well so much for statistics. I suggest you do your own summary of where you've met the relationships in your life. Then pursue those avenues that gave you the best results.

Getting to know each other

Having sorted out how you meet, it's time to take a look at how we can get to know each other.

Is there a natural way to connect and learn about each other that supports seeing each other as we really are, instead of the fantasy picture? Yes, I believe there is.

I've pondered this a lot. I came of age in the United States so I'm well versed in the ins and outs of the American system of dating. To my way of thinking dating is not a natural process for getting to know someone. On dates you get dressed up and go out to dinner, the movies, dancing and so on. On dates you rarely do the everyday activities that life is made up of. I believe a better way to get to know someone is to do the things you normally do, together.

Here are some examples. If you like walking or hiking, do that together. If you like hanging out over a cup of tea and philosophizing over the meaning of life, then do that together. If your passion is auto racing, then go do that together. Introduce each other to your hobbies and everyday activities, include each other when you get together with friends, and be curious about each other. Who are you in your most natural state?

I knew one couple that dated the standard American way. They were out and about to dinners, dancing, the movies and they went to lots of parties. Once they got married, they quit going out. Why? Because the husband wasn't interested in being out and about, he really loved staying home. But the courtship process had forced him to do things he really didn't care about and he had to pretend in order to get dates. Well, once he was married he no longer needed to do the courtship ritual. The wife was dismayed, because she really enjoyed the social life and being out and about. She was disappointed she had not known who she was marrying.

What I'm trying to say here is that by not engaging in your regular activities with potential mates there is a bigger chance that you won't find out who you are hooking up with.

The other aspect of this is as you explore common and uncommon interests you can meet where you intersect and let go of the rest. There are many ways to have relationships and there is no set structure anymore.

One way to explore who you are is to do the exercises in this book. Alone and then dialogue together. Remember the *talking dog* exercise early in the book? Use it to dialogue and it will be much easier to learn about each other.

The important thing is to be curious, to play detective. Find out what is important to the other person. Why do they care about the things they do? How did they get interested in their hobbies, how did they get started? Talk to each other, on the phone, via email, via snail mail.

I know one couple who live apart for long periods because their work takes them to different parts of the world. They stay in frequent contact via phone and email and actually talk to each other more when they live apart than when they were living together. They say it's like getting to know each other all over again and has put a new sparkle into their relationship. When you live together conversation easily becomes about practical stuff like picking up kids at day care or whose turn it is to fix dinner or clean the toilet. Research shows the average couple talks to each other abysmally few minutes per week.

Another couple I know has throughout their long marriage made Friday night date night. No matter what, Friday evening they have dinner with each other, no kids, no friends, just the two of them. Even if they only go to MacDonald's, they spend time with each other and talk. Very important!

Other aspects to explore as you get to know each other is talking about how you handle conflicts. What you do when you get angry or sad. What you expect from others when you are emotionally upset or sick? How was your family? What was it like growing up? and much more.

One of the best ways to find out how well you get along together is to go on an extended road trip. Being in such close quarters for a week or longer is bound to expose the real you. To make it really exciting, go visit and stay with friends, yours and theirs. I guarantee you'll know each other well after that. It's not enough to take a charter trip and park in a sun chair for a week. No you need an active vacation. Where you have to interact and resolve conflicts and live under stress. I know several couples who have done this before they decided to get married. One friend said after several months traveling through Nepal and other countries, she and her husband figured if they had managed to get along under those circumstances, they could manage to get along living together. Another couple I knew went on a camping trip, pitching tents and cooking over an open fire. I think it's a good test.

Bring them into your everyday life to be with you during your normal activities. Especially bring your friends together, see how they interact socially and otherwise. When you bring lovers into your normal life they may trigger your friends jealousies. If that happens, how do you choose? Who is more important? Your happiness or your soon to be former friend's possessiveness?

Expectations

When we walk into a relationship, we have expectations. Many of these are unspoken and it's a rare human who is aware of all his or her hidden agendas and subconscious expectations. If we can unearth the unspoken expectations, we can at least have a dialogue about them. It's when they come flying out in hurts and accusations that they are hard to deal with.

I think it's of value to think about what one is used to. Simply talking about how our families handled conflict, sickness and success. What was allowed and what wasn't. What were the basic values and attitudes you were brought up with and how do you agree or disagree with them? If your Mummy doted on you when you were sick and your partner's family treated illness like something where you shut yourself in your room by yourself until well, then you will have hurt feelings when one of you gets sick, because you have two very different images of what is supposed to happen.

Another big area that will surface when you get close to another, are unresolved hurts from the past. Getting them up into the open is the best way to move forward. Understanding the dynamics you bring into the relationships and being able to dialogue and work through them as they come up will enrich your relationship.

I would like to see therapy training focus on teaching skills for life, where you learn first of all how to get conscious and work with yourself, then practice your skills with the others in the group. You trade with each other and help each other grow. Can you imagine the potential in organizations and relationships if we were skilled in working with each other and could resolve ancient and current conflicts right then and there.

I have one therapy friend who is bringing this concept into her marriage. So far it's been hard work, but I think they will have a much deeper and richer relationship in the long run.

Speaking of marriage, it's an ancient ceremony that brings expectations and it's a rare person who doesn't go on autopilot when the wedding bells ring. There are unspoken beliefs that it's up to the man to bring in the money and the wife is to be obedient and so on. Many people let go once they are married. I've heard the comment more than once, "now I don't have to make an effort any more," meaning it's ok to walk around like a slob and not plan special outings or needing to be nice. Sounds like they are heading for disaster. Would you let your best friend treat you this way? Let alone a spouse? I don't think so!

I would rather know

If my mate is having affairs, I would rather know. Goes against what most people believe, but I really want to know who I am dealing with. That's the whole point of finding out about who the other person is. Rather than trying to squeeze them into my idea of how they should be, I would rather find out who they really are to begin with. It is the whole idea behind setting someone free – free to be themselves and loving him or her as they are.

If you meet someone who is a notorious womanizer, why not accept that that is who he is? No, what we typically do is demand that the poor man toe the line. Frequently he attracts the kind of woman who is jealous and suspicious so he can take maximum heat for doing what he most naturally does. Why not send him out with condoms with the admonition, "don't bring home any diseases?" Why not set the poor man free? Or, the woman, as the case may be.

Why is he or she out and about anyway? In couples where both feel that they have found the love of their life, that they are with the one they were meant to be with, the need for extramarital affairs seems to go away. There is no need to look outside the relationship. I can't say if this is always true, but it appears to be in many cases. However, most relationships aren't that way. Many would rather be with someone than be alone. And hey we might as well practice until Mr. or Ms. right walks in.

Love is not about control and manipulation, although some people seem to think so. Love is about acceptance and freedom. Perhaps this is such a hot topic for me as I've had boyfriends as well as women friends who have wanted to own me. I hate ownership. I get claustrophobic when someone tries to limit me. I withdraw when someone demands that I buy into his or her agenda.

Twenty-Five

Joyful moments exercise

Here is an exercise to help you get to know yourself and useful as a dialogue tool for couples and groups. I call it the *joyful moments* exercise. I came across it when I was working on career issues, really trying to understand what was important to me.

Get out some pen and paper and quiet yourself. You are going to focus your attention on happy moments in your life. Think back and ask yourself, start to ponder, what were the happiest moments in my life? What events do I remember most clearly? When did life seem to vibrate around me? When have I felt content and happy and in love with the world? What moments do I remember with joy in my heart?

Write down the events that come into your awareness. I was quite surprised when I did this exercise. All the things I had been taught should be important to me, you know big events like job promotions, marriage and buying a house, were not on the list of my joyful moments. No, it was simple things like playing on the see-saw with a friend and colleague, eating oranges and laughing, seeing the Christmas lights on Champs-Elysees, walking in the crunchy snow under a starlit sky, driving to work along the Seine early in the morning, making eye contact with a special friend, drinking tea with friends, smelling roses, or swimming in the sea. The most significant moments were not what I expected!

While rummaging through my files I found the original exercise I had done. I've included it here as I think it may help you to get started on your list:

Moments of pleasure, those special moments we remember. I thought I'd write this to get in touch with what I consider special, what is it that I really treasure in life, what is important and what is it that I remember.

- On the seesaw with my friend and colleague. Laughing, just enjoying the moment, feeling the soft warm breeze, enjoying the serenity of nature, the spontaneity of getting on the seesaw, the image of one of our co-workers seeing us - that sure looked like our managers - but it couldn't be, they are too serious and work dedicated to do that. The fun of playing, really innocent fun. We were eating oranges as we did this. Really good ones we had picked up in Orange. And I had a terrible cold, but it never bothered me when I was with my buddy.

- The excitement of taking the Hovercraft from Dover to Boulogne, the adventure, not having done it before, the satisfaction of I dared to do it.

- Soaking up the sun sitting on the ferry from Dieppe to Newhaven. Such peace and serenity. Again I was alone.

- Making love to one of my entity mates. The complete focus on each other. The way he ran his fingers through my hair, sang to me, danced with me, looked at me, and talked to me. So intense and so full of love. That complete surrounding of him and he wasn't preoccupied with anything else, and neither was I, it was so in the moment.

- Talking to a special man, making eye contact, happened a couple of times, the looking into each others eyes and sharing what was there, I was open to him looking into me, reading me, and he let me read him.

- Having astral sex, it was so full of love, so complete and whole and healing.

- Lover telling me he loved me in my pink curlers and fuzzy slippers in the morning.

- Walking in the fields, or woods, after it rains, it is so fresh and earthy smelling.

- The sound of snow, it gets so quiet.

- Eating hot dogs at Walters, with real mashed potatoes.

- Talking on the telephone and getting an aha about a concept or something going on in my life, like on the whole concept of Grace, discussing ideas freely just to explore them, try them on.

- Eating hot and sour soup and mongolian beef with best friend, special delivery from Hunan Harbor.

- The feeling of freedom of making my last condo mortgage payment.

- Eating steak, potato, little peas, béarnaise sauce and red wine, such happiness.

- Eating cherries and laughing and joking with all the guys, there must have been five of them in my office. We had such a loud good time our boss came and asked us to hold it down in there.

- Playing in the bubble bath in the morning, playing with the bubbles, making little animals.

- Not getting dressed all day, staying in bed or in bathrobe, reading, eating and sleeping.

- Talking and laughing with the secretaries, when the guys were out. Doing a rendition of Sur le pont d'Avignon complete with gestures.

- Dancing to the Heats with my dance buddy. That total letting go, enjoy, don't have to worry what you look like, just enjoy the music.

- Listening to Viennese music, the Strauss in particular, so happy.

- Seeing mists rise in the morning around the trees, over the Loire.

- An early morning walk on the beach at Sete by myself.

- Reading with ex, after we'd gone to the library to get stacks of books we'd curl up on the couch and read to each other.

- Having the sun wake me up in the morning.

- Seattle in the sunlight with the mountains so clear and the water so blue, it's one of the most breathtaking sights there is.

- Getting a hug from a male friend, so complete and so warm, and so sexual.

- Hugging my brother, feeling that total love, he gives real hugs.

- Singing, "all I want for Christmas is a well hung man" to the tune of "all I want for Christmas is my two front teeth" with best friend after she lay out hung on the Scrabble board.

So far none of these have to do with work or school, but some have to do with learning, many sensuality, spontaneity, bliss and nature.

- Hearing the sound of the surf at the beach.

- Playing in the water with friend and her kids.

- Riding horses and being around them when I was a kid.

- Seeing Paris in the morning light going to work.

- The pretty Christmas lights on the Champs Elysees.

- Fire works on Lake Union on the fourth of July.

More recently I had a very joyful moment when my first book came out. The euphoria and expansiveness I experienced when I held the real book in my hand was exquisite. It lasted for days, no weeks. Truly an extended joyful moment. I glowed! One friend exclaimed, "it must be better than sex" - no I don't think so, it's not the same but it's right up there with peak experiences.

Peak experiences

I didn't coin the term *peak experiences*. Regina Pontow did. I went to her workshop on resume writing, where I learned an exercise to discover your peak experience skills. I'll tell you about the basic premise and you can ponder your own peak experience skills.

Peak experience is another term for joyful moment. It occurs when you do something you really like, where time goes by without your notice. In this exercise it is connected with work type skills, but the clues can be found in childhood. What you are looking for are activities that you do naturally and with ease. Some kids build bridges, my brother would take radios apart and put them back together without any parts missing. I organized all my Barbie dolls and their clothes in neat wardrobes and used chocolate boxes to sort all the accessories. To this day I have a natural knack for organization. My mother says I never lost anything like most kids do, not even a mitten.

What games did you like to play? I liked to fantasize and I wrote plays. I organized a club one time. I went riding and loved hanging out at the stables. I daydreamed a lot. See the signs were there, I was born to be a writer and philosophizer. Daydreaming still comes naturally to me.

Anyway, in this exercise you pull together your peak experiences. Activities you love to do. Then you sort them by the type of skill that is involved. Within the activities you love to do, you will discover certain skills that you use over and over. When you get to use these skills at least 70% of the time in your job, you will be happy and fulfilled. The trick is to organize your work so you get to use your best skills.

For example my least favorite skill is sales and marketing. I am worthless at the traditional way of putting together sales letters, then following up with a telephone pitch to make an appointment for a sales call where you then have to sell yourself or your product. As a self-employed individual, I've had to find ways to market myself. I've had to get creative. As I get creative and ponder ways to connect with my customers, I've found ways to do this and stay sane.

Logic may dictate that I should focus on bookstores. I just can't find the energy to call store after store. But over time, I'm adding them one by one. Doing it at a natural pace works better for me, and I suspect I have a higher success rate this way. When the timing is right, they say yes.

What seems to work for me is to do a little bit of this and a little bit of that. A combination of talking to the press, updating my website, sending out a newsletter, calling on bookstores. This morning I was praying for guidance how to best market my first two books, in ways I may not have thought of. The answer came to get therapy and body work schools to use them in their courses, to have them available on their reading lists. Well of course, if I can get the therapy teachers to use my material, they will recommend my books to their pupils who in turn will recommend them to their clients.

Instead of resisting our least favorite activities, I believe we can grow if we find ways to accomplish the tasks, but in a way that suits us. In pursuing the marketing to therapy schools, I get to use one of my peak experience skills, which is learning. I get to go grazing for information to find the schools, then find the decision makers, then build relationships with them and so on. When I can incorporate my peak experience skills into tasks that are not natural for me, I can make a success of them too.

Twenty-Six

Right relationships

Having just gone through a Venus transit (June 8, 2004) there has been much discussion about what it means. One of the main themes I pick up on is the idea of right relationships - with myself and with others. I don't believe we are meant to be able to love everyone equally and I certainly don't buy the idea that being nice is always the best way to show love.

Anger and setting limits and boundaries is one way to show that you care and may at times be the most loving thing you can do for yourself and the other person.

I've found it useful to from time to time review my relationships. If I met this friend today, would I want to get to know him/her? Would I choose to spend time with them? Reflect on what you get from the relationship and what you put into it.

I don't think it's ever 50/50 in a relationship and I certainly don't want to keep score. No, what I am saying is to stop and reflect occasionally. Do I give more than what I get back? Or does the other person give more and I take more? What do we get from our connection? Does it feed my soul? Does it help me grow? How do I feel when I think of my friend? How well can we talk to each other? How do we handle conflicts?

The energy in a friendship has to flow both ways. Both have to give and receive. Reflect on who you want to hang out with and spend time with. And don't be afraid to set limits. If your friend is chewing on the same crap time and time again, it's really ok to say, "you've told me this before - is there something new you want to share with me?" It does help them to get on with it. Chewing on the same stuff over and over doesn't help anyone resolve it. Talking about things is important, but when it gets repetitive, you are stuck. Help each other get unstuck by speaking up.

Competition or cooperation?

How do you see the world? Do you believe in abundance, that there is more than enough for everybody to go around? Or do you believe in scarcity, that resources, money or jobs are limited and that there is not enough for everyone? Do you believe in competition or cooperation? Do you see your coworkers as threats to your career or as co-creators of something that is more than the sum of the parts?

Is your world one of free flow or restriction? Do you believe you can save yourself into prosperity? Of course you can't. This is one of the underlying reasons why so many corporations are failing today. Downsizing to slim a fat workforce may be useful once. Repeated downsizings to make the stock price go up are bound to fail in the long run. Stocks go up when your neighbor loses his job. Sooner or later it will be your turn.

How you look at yourself and others determines how you act in the world. Do you see your love interest as something to be won, someone to be yours, to belong only to you? Do you approach relationships and work from a have to have no matter what, or letting it come to you of its own free will?

I believe there is more than enough for everyone. I don't believe in competition. I don't believe in winners and losers. I believe there is space for everyone, there is love for everyone and there is work for everyone. If we listen to our Divine guidance, and allow Spirit to work through us, to show us our rightful place, we can't go wrong. It's when we covet that which does not belong to us, and scheme to get it, that all our troubles begin.

I love the writing of Florence Scovel Shinn and Emmet Fox. They explain so eloquently the principle of: that which belongs to us by Divine right, or by right of consciousness, is ours, we cannot lose it. It is guaranteed that we have it. We may not get what we think we want, but we always get what we need, when the time is right.

I've never understood the game of seduction. I don't understand the scheming, the hidden agendas, the lies and deception that are all part of that game. But then I learned, from a psychic and therapist, that seductive people are always hostile toward their partner.

In other words, seduction is the opposite of love. It's about anger that is not allowed to surface. It's about control. It's about manipulating the other person. It's about winning or losing. It's about one-upmanship, about showing who rules. It doesn't feel good.

Seduction is like a cat and mouse game. It's a hunt where you are chasing someone, you are hunting, you prey on the object of your seduction, see them as a trophy to be won or laid down. Once you catch it, you toy with it, torment it, just like a cat does with a mouse. What has love got to do with that?

Unearthing this tidbit of information, this jewel of insight, helps me understand some of the women who have been friends of mine. They would think nothing of seducing a man I was interested in. Not because they really wanted him, but only to show they could, or to make sure I would lose. With friends like that, who needs enemies?

It's been said that there really are only two basic emotions – love and fear. Perhaps it is more correct to say they are the underlying driver beneath any emotion. Whatever you feel, whatever you do, ask yourself if you are coming from love or fear. What is your underlying motivation?

If I want someone, I believe in being straight on. I like you. I am interested. I want to get to know you. If the feeling is mutual, wonderful, if it is not, it wasn't meant to be. If he isn't the Divine selection, why would I want him?

One of my favorite memories of the straight-on approach is from my University days. A classmate and I were really good friends. Without each other, we never would have made it through physics classes. One day, he shows up at my apartment and says, "it's been quite a while since I got laid, are you interested in coming home with me and having sex?" Very straightforward. Easy to deal with. No hidden agendas. I said yes. I hadn't had any for a while either. It was nice. We remained friends. It's relatively easy to keep it amicable, as long as you aren't in love with each other. Then it gets trickier, but if handled honestly and earnestly it will come out as it should in the end. As long as we don't script the ending, but let God sort the details, it will turn out for our highest good in the long run.

Twenty-Seven

I haven't been honest with myself

Yesterday I went to see our local psychic. I wanted to understand, not just release, the Brussels life and any other incarnations that were related. I also wanted to make sure that I had got it right. That I had made the appropriate rearrangements. I had. There were several more lifetimes involved, which explains why this was such a potent and deep issue with many components. She described the cleanout as a whirlwind or tornado where everything was sucked into the storm and the pieces flung out. At this point I was picking up the pieces that were meant to stay with me. The past was now released and we were truly finished with it.

But there were two things I realized I hadn't been honest with myself about. One is my feelings for the young man from Brussels. We are friends in this life and I keep telling myself that is ok. In truth I want him. I want to know his body, his mind, his heart and soul. Why is it so hard to be truthful with oneself? Is it because I don't want to make demands? or because I am afraid of rejection? or is it that I am afraid he'll be ashamed of me? Which leads me to the second realization.

I have been working every which way to release the fibroids in my sacral chakra region. I asked the psychic why they hadn't released yet on the physical. It turns out the causal point comes from a life in France in the 1400's. I was a young woman in that life who got pregnant without being married. Being an unwed mother in those days was a big sin and the church did everything to shame me. The child died in my womb sometime in the second trimester. I took on the belief system of the church, I bought their authority and felt guilt and shame.

We can work and work on an issue but it won't release until we get to the original knot. Then, as we get hold of the key thread it unravels right in front of our eyes. I have always felt that my fibroids were about emotions and beliefs put on me by others, that the emotions weren't coming from inside me but were imposed from the outside. I have experienced the pain and emotions, but not been able to release them completely. Now I know the origin of the emotions, thoughts and beliefs. Now I can dissolve those thought patterns into the light, hand them back to their source.

The psychic explained that the fibroids are like blisters of shame. The church has done tremendous damage to women, imposing shame on our most natural functions. The woman is blamed if a man finds her attractive and he can't resist her charms. Women are blamed for being seductive temptresses. If a man and woman end up in bed, it's the woman's fault. I've heard more than once, "I didn't really want this to happen." So why did he? The implication is that a man can't control his urges or hormones. What a crock of shit.

Anyway, I realize that I still carry a lot of shame around being a woman. It's been imposed and projected on me, but I have sucked it in and made it my own. I haven't been honest with myself that I feel shame about my behavior or my lusts. I try to be flippant about it, try to be brave and say, "yes I have done all these things, I have been with all these men, I love sex and I feel very lusty." But in all that I have hidden the shame from myself. Deep inside I don't feel ok about my womanness. Deep inside I feel shame. Because the church and other authority structures have made it very clear that it's not acceptable or approved of. Add to that all the witch hunts and the inquisition where basically all feminine traits were cause for being burned at the stake. So we women carry a heavy karmic burden of collective shame and fear. It is time to hand it back to its source and say, "no thank you, I don't think so."

Healing

What is brought into the light can be healed. That's the beauty of it. To be a woman means I have a right to be sexual, sensual, flirty, intuitive, creative, flowing and loving. There are very few women who feel free to be in full bloom. That is my next challenge, my next area of growth, to become the mature woman in full bloom. To bring out all my humanness in the dance of life.

When men and women are free to be their natural selves they are empowered. I really like the Hawaiian Huna philosophy. They don't have the same concept of sin as the western authority model. They do have several *do nots* in their code of forgiveness:

• to miss the path, to err by omission

• to go overboard

• to do excess

• to do intentional harm to someone with hate in mind

Quite a different approach than we are used to. Their whole way of life is about following the path of highest life energy. I like that. I think we were all meant to be alive with joy and pleasure as well as pain and sadness. That all aspects of being human need to play a part in our lives.

We are meant to be free of restricting and controlling minds who want to dictate our every action. When I am free they have no power over me. Yes, *freedom*, that was the last shout from William Wallace in the movie Braveheart. They may try to kill us, but they can never take away our souls and our inner freedom. It's interesting how many world leaders have found their strength while incarcerated in prison. Food for thought. The light gets stronger when the darkness closes in.

Freedom. Be free, be brave and follow your inner guidance. Let yourself live life. Try something new. Make mistakes. Be here now. What are you waiting for?

Twenty-Eight

Lifting the curse

Another restless night. I get up to do Sylvia Browne's regression once more. I want to get to the bottom of my "sin" and heal the curse of the church. As I go back in time, first to age twenty in this life, I revisit my time with Jerry, where the church he belonged to drilled home the message that women were less than men, at age ten I revisit another shaming experience, then at conception I meet up with my twin sister who then opted out of being born. My twin helps me understand that my most important mission in this life is to heal the guilt and shame and to help myself and all women to be free of the curse of sin, to lift the curse of womanhood.

As I travel backward in time, the regression leads me straight to France, the Abbey of St. Maur to be exact and the year is 1401. My name is Clarisse, a young woman of 22 with long black curly hair and green eyes. I have committed the mortal sin of getting pregnant, allowing a man to come into me while still a maiden, not yet married. The young man from the Brussels life is there too, he is my brother and a great comfort and support to me.

There is a leader in the church who curses me and I take on the whole belief system of sin. That I have done wrong. That it is entirely my fault as a woman that the man could not control himself and I bear the entire blame for the child that is growing in my belly.

I seek solace in the church, praying for help to be "good" and "pure." In that life I lived and died in shame. In this current life, I had come across the cross of St. Maur about the time all these past lives started to unravel. I bought a pendant and have been wearing it every day since.

The dilemma for believers is that God is all good. God does not punish or believe in sin. It is a human construct. The church has made up the idea of sin to keep the flock under control. But sin is not real. Yes we feel the condemnation, but in the eyes of God, sin does not exist. It only exists in the minds of people who hate.

Eve in the Garden of Eden

It's perhaps not a coincidence that for the past six years I have lived in a place called Paradise. Lots of jokes come my way about Eva in Paradise, quite often with a quip of "where's Adam?" I'd like to know that too. Who is to be number 51? Only time will tell. And perhaps I won't tell and keep it a private matter. My next writing venture feels like it could be fiction, storytelling, spinning new possibilities in the web of life.

Eve, according to the church, was the original sinner. She was the temptress who offered Adam a taste of the apple, of knowledge. Eve, through her actions, caused the fall of man. Poppycock on that interpretation. They would like us to believe that all women are sinful and the poor men are incapable of making decisions while under the spell of a woman.

Who made this up? Why do we swallow it hook, line and sinker? Why do we buy this philosophy that only cause us feel bad about ourselves? Why do we let some dried up fart dictate to us how to live? Someone, who bets are hasn't been laid in a long while. Why do we think life on earth is about punishment and denying our humanness?

I believe we are all here to be human, to experience all that earth has to offer. We already are spiritual beings. There is no need to purify or to lift ourselves above. We are here to be human, to be grounded in physical reality. That means enjoying the fruits of the earth - like wine, food and good company. It means exploring all the nuances of relationships and tasting all that the body has to offer through the sexual and other sensory experiences.

We are here to be creative, to dance and sing and to enjoy life. Look around, how many people are living here and now, truly savoring the experience? No we struggle, we get caught up in mental constructs that don't mean a thing in the end.

On the other hand, we now have the ability to heal past life wounds in a way we didn't have access to previously. This means there are many of us on the healing path. There is a lot of pain that is being released through this healing work and that is very good. The trick is to move on once the healing has taken place and go for the gusto, go for life, go for pleasure, go for exploration of what it really means to be human, all flesh and blood. When we die we return to the spirit plane, where all the earth experiences are not possible. There we are pure spirit and there we can spend endless time in bliss in the light.

While we are on earth we have a different purpose. It's called to live. To live life to the best of our ability. God makes no judgments. Only people judge.

Righteous Anger

Getting in touch with righteous anger is one of the key healing elements to throw off abuse and other shaming projections. Until we get angry and punch back, so to speak, the other person remains in a power over situation. To be empowered we need to take a stand, express our feelings and at times really let it rip.

I have behaved uncharacteristically of late. Instead of being so understanding and therapeutic, I've let myself react like a flesh and blood human being. The person who was my father in the Brussels life had acted out similar behavior in this life. I started out by pointing out the present behavior, then added it's not just about me to the full blown this is how I feel when I discovered the whole past life connection. Throughout it all the other person reacted with, "it's all your problem and it would benefit our relationship if you sorted it."

It never is just about me. That's the lesson I learned. I really let it rip and let the other person have it. It felt really good. I kicked the "father" out of my life for good. I feel really free. Lots of energy and emotions have released in the process, and I believe that by completing that aspect, I got access to the France life in the 1400's.

Twenty-Nine

I take my orders from Spirit

By now you've probably gathered that I get my orders from within. I meditate every day and ask for guidance from my Higher Self. I have learned to trust her direction. Our Higher Selves have a much broader perspective than we do. They can see farther and they are connected to all the other Higher Selves. They want what is best for us. Sometimes the guidance won't make sense, because we don't have all the pieces of the puzzle, yet.

When we can learn to let go and take action as directed by Spirit, we allow magic to flow in our lives. Practicing on the small decisions will help you to tackle the bigger ones. I signed the contract for the publication of this book before it was finished. I knew it was the right thing to do and the timing was given to me as well. A few weeks later I was guided to give notice on the house I am renting. I will be moving right after I send in this manuscript to the publisher. At this moment, I don't know where I am moving to, what I will be doing there nor any other details. I do know it will be revealed to me when the time is right. I am very calm and feel more settled after the decisions were made than before.

By letting go of my house, I create space for something new to come in. I was meant to write three books here, I think of them as *the Paradise Trilogy*. The next place will have new contacts and new challenges. I learned a long time ago that wherever Spirit sends you, you will make the connections you are meant to make and you will have the experiences you are meant to have. What you thought it was all about may not be it at all, but rest assured that in the long run your Higher Self loves you and wants you to grow.

So again the message is to *let go and let God*.

I have an inner sense of excitement and adventure. Where will I go next and explore? I feel alive with expectant possibilities. The other day a friend called and was reminiscing how it was when I arrived back in Sweden, how fun it had been to play tourist with me in Stockholm. I think the universe sends us these messages so we can remember our earlier successes and to remind us of the fun in not knowing where you are going.

I have been getting messages about moving for some time, but had been running into roadblocks. The universe was clearly messaging that the time wasn't right yet. Then one morning I woke up, clear as a bell, today I send in my notice on the house. When the decision has ripened, it's easy, and it all flows.

Difficulties

Writing this book is at times quite difficult. My life seems to either be intense activity followed by periods of sitting and staring into space. I suppose that is how it's meant to be at the moment.

I reflect on how the main subject matters in this book - organizations and relationships - are subjects I either know a lot about or have pondered a lot, yet while I am writing this book, the absence of both is making itself painfully known. Perhaps this is why it's so hard to write. I am reminded with every word of what I am missing.

Many of my friends have like me spent many years on our personal growth. We have talked about how ten or fifteen years ago we all had good jobs, owned our homes and had relationships. Now we have none of that and have dug deep into ourselves. What was the point of it all? At least some of us had the expectation that there would be a reward at the end of the rainbow.

Is there really a meaning to life? Is there really a purpose? I sense that I am doing important work, for myself and others. But why are so many of us doing so poorly economically and relationally? One friend finally got a job, after many years of unemployment, only to discover her new boss wanted her accounting skills for tax evasion purposes.

Another friend finally found a man, only to discover he was a psychopath. Quite a few of my women friends say they would just as soon live by themselves, they are so disappointed in the men they have met that it's simply not worth the bother. That feels depressing. There has got to be a point to it all.

At the same time I have small successes. Newspapers and magazines write about me. Bookstore buyers tell me my books look interesting and they put them on the shelves of their stores. Readers of my books give me positive feedback. So in many ways good things are happening.

I suppose the molasses effect I'm experiencing at the moment is mainly due to my own fears. So many times I've tried to go out with my ideas about organizations and relationships only to be met with fear, criticism, non-interest or downright ridicule. So it's no wonder I'm reluctant to finish this work to put myself out there to be screamed at. That's it isn't it? The memory of being screamed at. The memory of being ragged on about how my ideas are not the norm and that I can't do it this way, I'm not an expert, my ideas threaten - hmmm - threaten who?

Yes, my ideas have threatened various friends before. I've been screamed at and pounded back into silence. But you know what? I refuse to be silent anymore. I will be heard and I will put my ideas out there. They aren't cast in stone but I think they can be of help to many to sort and ponder how we may do organizations and relationships that actually work. The way we do things today certainly isn't cutting the mustard.

My woman friend who encountered a psychopath was told by him that she must obey him. What weird ideas do we carry around about how we should be when we get together with another?

We have so many built in ideas, or pictures of how it should look. We expect to fall in love with someone our age, and in walks someone much older or younger. Just to stir our issues and about the time we are working through ageing stuff.

Life isn't just a dance on roses. It consists of ups and downs, failures and successes. Sometimes we are euphoric, sometimes we just stare into space, sometimes we feel murderous, sometimes we are sad and sometimes we feel happy. It's all part of life. The difficulties come when we have extended periods of trials, where it's hard to see a light at the end of the tunnel. That's when it's most difficult to keep going, to keep the belief up that it's all worth it. But you have to keep trying all the same.

As I was going through the healing process around the issues from my life in Brussels in the 1700's I hit a particularly difficult spot. I shared with a friend, who was also going through a dark place, that if I didn't believe all this work was worth it and that in the end it would get better, I would go drown myself right now. She said, "at least you don't have to go far, since you live close to a lake." Humor helps to lighten the load. We made a pact, that before we would do any drowning, we could call each other and then have a hell of a party with all our friends. We surmised that by then we would feel like living again. More of our friends have joined our drowning-party pact. I think it helps to keep us sane and it makes it ok to say, "right now my life is hell." I think that is one of the difficulties when you feel like life isn't worth living, there is such a taboo to even utter the thought, let alone experience the feeling.

According to Per Hjalmar Svae of Norway who wrote *The Five Ego Patterns*, the way to heal feelings of not wanting to live is to allow ourselves to feel them. Each time we connect with the feeling that life isn't worth living we heal it a little more. The first time we reconnect with the emotion it may feel overwhelming and last for days. With each occurrence it becomes easier to be with the feeling, it doesn't last as long and eventually the emotion is healed. There is a very key distinction between feeling suicidal - we all do at one point or another – and acting on those feelings. The act of attempted suicide is a different emotion, it is destructive and most often it is a cry for help. Just helping to bring it out into the open to make it ok to have the emotion does much to help the process of healing.

When my friends and I acknowledged how we truly felt and made it ok to feel that way and created a way to connect and support each other when the going gets rough, we helped to heal ourselves and each other. Deep inside we know if we got this far we can make it in this life too. If you experience emotions that feel overwhelming, get help, from professionals and from friends and family. Building a support network before the sea gets rough is even better.

Life is a treasure hunt

They say that most successful entrepreneurs have some really big failures behind them. It's not unusual for them to have a bankruptcy or some other big mess-up before the big success comes. I'm sure they would tell us they learned from the mistakes. We learn from our failures what didn't work. Maybe it would be appropriate to say that life is a crapshoot? Or was my friend right when she said *life is a treasure hunt*?

If you look at life like a treasure hunt, then you don't have to have the answers. You are on a mission of discovery. You can explore and make mistakes. The universe is ever changing and so are we. Looking at life like a treasure hunt allows you to keep learning, to try different things, to explore and keep a level of excitement about what you are doing.

I like that. When I can explore my subjects from a treasure hunt perspective, I stay alive in the process. Whenever I try to teach from a viewpoint of "this is how it is," my writing goes static, because knowledge is not cast in stone. The moment I share an idea with you, it gets your grey cells churning, and you take off with an offshoot of my idea. So there is no static learning or knowledge. Knowledge is like fresh produce, it's not something that can sit on the shelf forever and stay the same.

Anytime you do one of my exercises, you add to the learning. You improve on what is already there. You make new discoveries. And that is how it should be. I would love to have your feedback in years to come from using the material in this book.

Thirty

Morning has broken

As I watch the sun come up over lake Wixen for the first time in months, bathing the sky with the sheer rose color of a an August dawn, with remnants of mists in between the trees, I feel the connection between signs in nature and my own process once again. This summer has been the rainiest in a hundred years, appropriate for spending time indoors completing this book.

The past life I had in Brussels three hundred years ago has been working its way through. Although the events happened a long time ago, the emotions are experienced as now until healed. It's been excruciatingly painful at times and difficult beyond belief as I reconnect with lost parts of myself.

I am extremely grateful to my friends who have put up with and helped me through these difficulties, for listening, offering advice and most of all for being there. Without this emotional support system I wouldn't have come through it nor been able to allow the material to surface and heal. My gratitude to my dear friends overflows with love and many heartfelt thanks.

Yesterday I first experienced a very fidgety energy, restless, wanting to do. As I centered myself to see what was percolating beneath the push for action I connected with a frustration. Letting myself soften into the feeling, focusing on the physical sensation in my solar plexus, more exactly the liver, tears arose and released. I felt anger, frustration and sadness all at the same time. That sorted, I went about my day.

Later on in the afternoon I sat, simply sat, and an incredibly deep sadness welled up from my sacral region. I reconnected with the love I felt for the man I lost in Brussels, and I reconnected with the love he felt for me. I was aware in every cell of my body how it felt to be loved and how much I had loved him. It was very powerful, to experience the positive aspects of love, to feel that deep connectedness. When I lost him, I felt as if I had lost myself, he was that much a part of me. On a soul level, that love will always be there. In my earth lives since, I have been disconnected from those feelings for nearly three hundred years, so you can imagine it was powerful. It is so sweet to reconnect to heart love that is connected to the physical and spiritual love.

I wrote a lot about my longing to connect physically, emotionally, mentally and spiritually with a man in my second book. Little did I understand how disconnected my own parts were. During the night I have been awake with a lovely sensuality in my body that has been long absent. The years I've spent working through my emotional pains have been painfully absent in relationships and sexual experiences. I've had close friends, yes, and have learned how to build an emotional support system.

Before I started to work on my emotional issues, I had lots of sexual experiences, but they were not so emotionally connected. Now I understand why I was unable to and why I've had to connect up my parts in sections. If I had tried to be present sexually, physically, emotionally, mentally and spiritually all at the same time, I would have blown a fuse. So the universe sets it up perfectly so we can uncork one aspect at a time. Then, finally, integration comes. The emotions I have experienced in reconnecting with the Brussels life have been so intense, if they had come sooner, or while in relationship, I doubt I could have coped. I needed to surface and release them so I could handle the energy of being in a twosome with all of me.

Presence is being human

When I talk about being present, I really mean that we need to allow ourselves to be human and in our bodies. It means we get to be pouty, or bouncy or sad. It means that when we have sex it won't always be wonderful, it may bring up anger or other feelings we think aren't allowed, but the more we let it rip, so to speak, the more human we become. The trick is to catch all our mental beliefs about how it should be and lifting the lid just a tad to let the real me and you come out. That's really what love is. To be human.

To be human involves feeling all emotions, whether "nice" or not. The father from the Brussels life has awakened some very dark and murky emotions in me, and that is appropriate. I feel vengeful and spiteful,

I feel vicious, and afraid all at the same time. I experience panic and deep fear that the "father" is spreading insinuations about me, like I am mentally ill or have totally lost it. I feel panicked at being attacked, or meeting another "friend" who is not at all who they appear to be, who is out to manipulate and control me, someone I can't trust. I feel intense murderous anger. I imagine doing all kinds of physical violence as I experience this deep rage. I get really furious with God "I deserve happiness, I deserve to be loved, I am so angry and pissed at you for allowing this to happen!"

Yes it is ok to feel angry with God too. I feel panic about where I'm to go, panic that I won't know what to do. The feeling is familiar that I won't have a place to go. I'm sure I experienced that feeling in Brussels, it's like being in prison, you are stuck with no way out.

Yet the spiritual side of me understands that in order to appreciate and know goodness, evil must be allowed to exist. It's funny that a close friend of mine sent me the Yogananda book on why God permits evil for a Christmas present last year. Divine timing I would say. If we didn't have evil, we wouldn't know how good good is, and we would neither appreciate it nor seek it out. We do grow by experiencing opposites and contrasts. If we experience the same thing all the time, we tend not to appreciate it and we don't grow much when life gets too routine. That's when we tend to lose the zest for life.

Life imitates life

If we pay attention to what books come our way and what television shows we watch we can see how life imitates life. We can then try to understand how the themes in them reflect our experience of life. Prior to doing the regression that unearthed the Brussels life, I had been watching a reality game show called *Paradise Hotel*. I couldn't for the life of me understand my morbid fascination with this show. Well it's all about deceit and treachery, playing games behind each other's backs in order to "win." So it was very appropriate indeed. By watching the show it focused my awareness on the issues that were up in my life and helped me understand another aspect of life.

One book I read this summer was about two girlfriends who spent their lives competing with each other. If one said, "I like that boy" the other one would connive to seduce him. When one wanted a part in a play, the other one schemed to be selected. Not because she was interested in acting. No it was out of spite, out of getting something the other one wanted. With friends like that who needs enemies?

Another book I read was about a man who appeared to be a model citizen in a small town, until his past caught up with him. As a youth he had raped and murdered a girl, fled and managed to change his identity. The wife hadn't a clue who she was married to. When he was arrested he said, "but I'm not the same person now." As the wife investigated what had actually happened she understood that he hadn't healed. He hadn't changed at all.

Only last weekend I watched a two part series about a Prussian king, his sister, her lover and his commander. The king and commander were so jealous of the love affair that they stopped at nothing to keep the star crossed lovers apart. It was an incredible testament to how far humans will go to force their will upon another, without regard to what was right or wrong. The destructiveness they played out was horrifying. In the very end the king allowed the lovers to be free, but they had to leave the country. I watched in morbid fascination. I needed to understand what drives people to get so blinded by their possessiveness that they have no qualms about destroying the very thing they claim to love.

It feels as if the drive to possess is fueled by hate, not love. What often happens in abusive relationships is when the game is up and the abused partner leaves, the abuser thinks, "if I can't have you, then I will make sure nobody else will." This is when they are most dangerous, because they would rather kill you than set you free. What's love got to do with that? Nothing, not a thing.

We all experience jealousy and envy at some point in life. I had a bout with feeling intensely angry at the success of another therapist. My rational mind knew I was being totally illogical, that the clients that went to her weren't mine. But I felt left out. I felt like I wasn't seen. I didn't feel valued. I felt very jealous and envious of the other therapist's apparent ease in making her practice thrive. I let my emotions out in therapy. The crazy thing about the experience is I really liked the therapist I was jealous of. But in order to heal I had to let myself feel the feelings, and acknowledge that I did indeed have them. Yes, to let myself be human. I suspect it's when we try to pretend we don't have those murky feelings that we tend to act them out. Which only causes more problems.

My heart overflows

A few days have passed. My awareness has totally shifted. I feel so grateful and I see such beauty that my heart overflows. Last night I dreamt that my dresses needed ironing so that is what I have been doing this morning. I put on heart music by the opera singer Barbara Hendricks. Her rendition of Ave Maria touches my heart in an even deeper way today. My heart opens and I feel the beauty, the love and I am so aware of how beautiful everything is. Looking out the window it is so beautiful, the butterflies, the flowers, the trees, the lake and the sun.

I am amazed there are so many more tears in me. But this time it's about gratitude, an appreciation of life and a deep thankfulness of all that I have let go of. Even though the last few months have been the most difficult in my entire journey I am so incredibly grateful that I finally got to the bottom of that barrel. I am done with the experience of friends and others who are out to sabotage my life. Now I am free to love and create a whole new life in love.

There is such love flowing into my heart that tears spill over. I marvel at how I have cried in sadness, in fear, in anger, in guilt and how wonderful it now is to cry because life is so beautiful. Yes this is how it was meant to be. I breathe easier as my joy tears cleanse my heart. Crying because life is so beautiful. I sure have been the sniffle lady this summer. In tune with Mother Nature. But I am so happy to be crying for joy, it is such a shift. There has been such murkiness to work through and now it is light. At times I've wondered if I'd ever get here and now I feel so full, of love and life. Thank you God, thank you nature, thank you all my friends here on earth and on the other side. I love you all.

It is appropriate that I move from here at the close of this book. This house has been a healing place emotionally and physically. Now it's time to go out in the world on another treasure hunt.

I write, I paint, I travel

It was hard enough to write this book the first time around. The book turned out to be one long ode to my longing for connectedness, in a relationship and in a larger organizational context. The writing helped me own how much I longed for those connections. Writing about it shifted my perspective and released my need for having them in my life. In a way it's weird to write about something that isn't in your life. On the other hand, the not having it sharpens your feelings and beliefs about it.

Working on this second edition some six years later is an odd experience. A love relationship has not knocked at my door, nor am I working in an organization. I've come to accept that it's meant to be this way. I've come to feel quite ok about it. Most people think I lead a fantastic life. I write, I paint, I travel. Alone. I've grown to like it. At times it's tedious to always be the one in charge, of everything. But for the most part I'm content to have it this way.

Today, a hedgehog appeared in my yard. Hmm what message have you brought,? I wondered. Grabbing the *Animal Speak* book, it says:

> Let love into your life. It's time to open your heart.
> Your gift is to give and receive love.

Funny how the universe works. I'd reworked the entire book but this last chapter had me stuck. Until now. Like a finishing crown upon the works. I have no idea what's in store for me. Perhaps a change is in the air? Typical though for life to take a turn when you least expect it.

Personal growth with a human touch

Eva Dillner is a writer, artist, therapist and teacher specializing in creative and therapeutic processes for inspiration and transformation. Through her company Divine Design she publishes books and art as well as audio and e-books. Her publishing partners are on the leading edge of the digital age.

Eva's art has been described as magical, mystical, dreamy, inspiring, fantastic, emotional, healing, like stars being born, a journey through Cosmos and Mother Earth.

In between writing and painting she travels and does the occasional exhibition or workshop, somewhere in the world.

See her website

www.divinedesign.nu

to catch up on the latest

www.ingramcontent.com/pod-product-compliance
Lightning Source LLC
Chambersburg PA
CBHW030300130626
46549CB00002B/628